Hatch Chile Cookbook

Gloria Chadwick

Pueblo Publishing

Hatch Chile Cookbook

© 2012 by Gloria Chadwick

Publisher's Cataloging-in-Publication Data

Chadwick, Gloria

Hatch Chile Cookbook

1. Hatch Chiles (Tex-Mex)
2. Cookery, American—Southwest   I. Title

ISBN 10: 1-883717-52-3

ISBN 13: 978-1-883717-52-0

Pueblo Publishing
Southwest Cookbooks

http://pueblopublishing.blogspot.com

For more Hatch chile recipes, visit
http://hatchchile.blogspot.com

For all Hatch Chile lovers...

May the recipes take you to a warm and wonderful place in Hatch Chile Heaven.

Contents

Introduction

I fell totally, completely, absolutely in love with Hatch green chiles at first bite. I'd gone grocery shopping one Saturday morning in August and was greeted by a wonderful aroma of freshly roasted Hatch green chiles wafting through the air. Of course I was curious and asked what was going on with the roasters outside the grocery store. Then I was treated to my first bite of Hatch chiles.

OMG. I felt as if I was in Hatch chile heaven. I began putting them into everything I made and creating recipes to feature them. I created a foodie blog devoted to this delicious chile and started posting recipes as well as gathering recipes from other foodies. It was a small leap from foodie blog to writing a cookbook devoted to Hatch green chiles.

 Look for the Hatch Chile Helper running through the pages and appearing on various recipes, offering helpful hints, spicy suggestions, and tasty tidbits.

You'll also find interesting information and fun facts on the city of Hatch and Hatch chiles. Look for the talking cactus in the pages.

Most of the recipes in this cookbook feature roasted Hatch chiles. You can buy them roasted or roast them yourself. (See the next paragraph.) If you've run out of your Hatch chiles stash, you can substitute other chiles, such as an Anaheim (which is closely related to Hatch chiles) or a poblano; if push comes to shove, you can use canned Hatch chiles.

There are several ways to roast chiles—broiler, stove-top, skillet, or grill. Preheat the broiler. Place the chiles under the broiler for six to eight minutes or until the skin blackens and blisters. For a gas stove, place the chiles directly on the flame, turning with tongs as the skin blackens and blisters; for an electric stove, place a skillet over high heat then add the chiles. Turn until they blacken and blister. Probably the best way is to roast chiles over the fire on a grill for the most authentic flavor.

When the chiles are blackened and blistered, place them in a plastic Zip-lock bag, seal it and let them steam for ten minutes. Remove the char, then stem and seed the chiles. Use them right away in a recipe or freeze them for later use. Some people remove the char before freezing, but then you run into the danger of freezer burn on your chiles. Depending on how many chiles you've bought to last you until the next harvest, keep in mind that the chiles get hotter in the freezer the longer they're in there.

Enjoy all the recipes in this cookbook and be sure to visit my Hatch Chile Heaven blog at **http://hatchchile.blogspot.com** for more recipes...

Appetizers

Cheese Rolls

Slice and serve on crackers. Or roll into a ball instead of a log and serve with tortilla chips.

    2 (8 oz.) packages cream cheese, softened
    1 cup shredded sharp Cheddar cheese
    1 medium avocado, peeled, pitted, and mashed
    1/4 cup finely minced onion
    1 tsp. garlic powder
    2 Hatch green chiles, roasted, peeled,
        stemmed, seeded, and finely chopped
    1 T. paprika
    1/2 cup finely chopped pecans or walnuts
    Crackers or tortilla chips

Combine the cream cheese and Cheddar cheese in a medium-size bowl.

Mix in the avocado, onion, garlic powder, and chiles.

Roll into two logs or shape into a ball. Sprinkle with paprika, then coat with the nuts.

Wrap in plastic wrap and refrigerate overnight.

Serve with crackers or tortilla chips.

Cheese Ball

Easy to make and even easier to eat.

1 (8 oz.) package cream cheese, softened
1 cup shredded Colby Jack cheese
2 Hatch green chiles, roasted, peeled,
    stemmed, seeded, and finely chopped
1/4 cup finely chopped red onion
1 tsp. Tabasco sauce
1/2 cup chopped red bell pepper
8 to 10 cilantro leaves
Tortilla chips

Combine the cream cheese, Colby Jack cheese, chiles, onion, and Tabasco sauce in a medium-size bowl.

Shape into a ball and roll in the chopped red bell pepper.

Wrap in plastic wrap and chill for several hours. Place on a bed of cilantro leaves. Serve with tortilla chips.

 Use Cheddar cheese instead of Colby Jack or use a combination of Cheddar and Monterey Jack cheeses. Roll in pecans or walnuts instead of the bell pepper.

Beef Chile Chimichangas

Chimichangas are little tortilla packets filled with beef, chicken, or cheese that are fried or baked until crisp.

1 pound lean ground beef
1 tsp. ground cumin
1 tsp. dried oregano
3 T. chili powder
1 tsp. black pepper
1 garlic clove, crushed
2 Hatch green chiles, roasted, peeled, stemmed, seeded, and chopped
1/4 cup sour cream
1/2 cup butter
8 (8-inch) flour tortillas
1 cup shredded Cheddar cheese

Preheat the oven to 500 degrees.

Brown the ground beef in a 12-inch skillet over medium heat. Season with the cumin, oregano, chili powder, pepper, garlic, and chiles while the meat is cooking.

Remove the pan from the heat and stir in the sour cream.

Melt the butter in a separate 10-inch skillet over medium heat. Using tongs, dip both sides of each tortilla in the butter. Drain off the excess.

Place 1/3 cup of the filling in the center of each tortilla. Fold the tortillas into square packets by folding in both sides over the filling and then folding over twice. Place seam side down in a 13 x 9 glass baking dish. Bake for 15 minutes or until crisp.

Remove from the oven and sprinkle with cheese. Return to the oven and bake for 5 more minutes to melt the cheese.

Hatch Hummus

Serve this with an assortment of chopped fresh veggies...
broccoli, cauliflower, cherry tomatoes, celery and carrot sticks,
crackers, and/or tortilla chips.

  1 (15 oz.) can chickpeas, drained and rinsed
  2 Hatch green chiles, roasted, peeled,
    stemmed, seeded, and chopped
  1/4 cup extra-virgin olive oil
  3 T. fresh lemon juice
  2 T. tahini (sesame paste)
  1 T. chopped cilantro
  2 garlic cloves, peeled
  1/2 tsp. salt
  1/2 tsp. ground cumin
  4 T. water

Combine all the ingredients in a blender or a food processor.
Blend on low speed until smooth, stopping frequently to push down
the ingredients. Add more oil if the mixture seems dry.

Place in a serving bowl. Serve with fresh veggies and crackers
or chips.

Sausage-Stuffed Mushrooms

Creamy and cheesy, these will practically melt in your mouth.

1 pound pork sausage
1 bunch green onions, chopped
2 to 3 Hatch chiles, roasted, peeled,
   stemmed, seeded, and chopped
1 (8 oz.) package cream cheese,
   cut into small chunks
1/2 cup grated Parmesan cheese
1 cup shredded Pepper Jack cheese, divided
2 pounds portobello mushrooms,
   stems removed and cleaned

Preheat the oven to 350 degrees. Lightly spray a 13 x 9 glass baking dish with nonstick cooking spray. Set aside.

Brown the sausage with the onions and chiles in a 12-inch skillet over high heat. Drain.

Remove the pan from the heat and add the cream cheese. Let soften from the residual heat, then stir to mix.

Add the Parmesan cheese and half the Pepper Jack cheese. Stir to mix, then spoon into the mushroom caps.

Place in the prepared baking dish and cook for 30 minutes or until the mushrooms have released their moisture.

Remove from the oven and sprinkle with the remaining cheese. Return to the oven and bake for 5 more minutes or until the cheese is melted.

Tex-Mex Bean Dip

It's amazing what you can do with a can of beans.

1 (16 oz.) can refried beans
1 (1.25 oz.) package taco seasoning mix
1/4 tsp. Tabasco sauce
1 (8 oz.) container sour cream
2 Hatch green chiles, roasted, peeled,
    stemmed, seeded, and chopped
1/2 cup diced avocado
1 cup shredded Cheddar cheese
1/2 cup diced green onion
1 medium tomato, chopped
Nachos, Doritos, or Tortilla chips

Combine the beans with the taco seasoning and Tabasco sauce in a medium-size bowl.

Spread the bean mixture on a serving platter.

Spread the sour cream over the top of the bean mixture.

Layer the chiles, avocado, cheese, onion, and tomato over the sour cream.

Cover and refrigerate for at least 4 hours.

Serve with your choice of chips.

Hot Black Bean Dip

While this is a dip, it's also good as a side dish.

1 T. vegetable oil
1/2 cup diced onion
2 garlic cloves, minced
1/4 cup Hatch green chiles, roasted, peeled,
    stemmed, seeded, and finely chopped
1/2 cup frozen corn, thawed
1 tsp. ground cumin
1/2 tsp. chili powder
1 (15 oz.) can black beans, drained and rinsed
1 cup shredded Monterey Jack cheese
Tortilla chips

Preheat the oven to 375 degrees. Lightly spray a 13 x 9 glass baking dish with nonstick cooking spray. Set aside.

Heat the oil in a 12-inch skillet over medium heat. Add the onion and sauté until tender.

Add the garlic, chiles, corn, cumin, and chili powder. Sauté for 2 to 3 more minutes.

Add the beans. Sauté for 3 to 4 more minutes. Mash about half the beans while cooking.

Place in the prepared baking dish. Top with the cheese and bake for 15 minutes or until the cheese is melted and lightly brown. Serve hot with tortilla chips.

Layered Dip

This is the perfect party dip.

1 (16 oz.) can refried beans
4 avocados, peeled and pitted
1 T. fresh lemon juice
1 (8 oz.) container sour cream
3 Hatch green chiles, roasted, peeled,
    stemmed, seeded, and finely chopped
1 cup shredded Monterey Jack cheese
1 cup shredded Cheddar cheese
1/2 cup chopped green onion
1 medium tomato, chopped
1 (2.25 oz.) can chopped black olives
Tortilla chips

Spread the refried beans in a 9 x 9 glass baking dish.

Scoop out the avocado pulp with a spoon and mash it in a small bowl. Mix in the lemon juice. Spread over the refried beans.

Mix the sour cream with the chiles in a separate small bowl. Spread this over the avocado layer.

Sprinkle the Monterey Jack and Cheddar cheeses over the top of the sour cream-chile mixture.

Top with the onion, tomato, and olives. Serve with tortilla chips.

Refried Bean Dip

Warmed in the microwave, all the ingredients blend their flavors for a delicious dip.

1 (16 oz.) can refried beans
1/2 cup shredded Monterey Jack cheese
1/2 cup shredded Cheddar cheese
1/2 cup Hatch green chiles, roasted, peeled,
 stemmed, seeded, and finely chopped
2. T. minced onion
1-1/2 tsp. chili powder
1/4 tsp. ground cumin
Tortilla chips

Place the beans, both cheeses, chiles, onion, chili powder, and cumin in a microwave-safe bowl. Heat on medium for 2 to 3 minutes, stirring once or twice to blend the flavors.

Serve warm or at room temperature with tortilla chips.

Green Chile Dip

Creamy and smooth, this blended dip is delicious.

2 Hatch green chiles, roasted, peeled,
 stemmed, seeded, and chopped
1 small onion, chopped
1 avocado, peeled, pitted, and chopped
1 (4 oz.) package cream cheese, softened
1/4 tsp. ground cumin
Tortilla chips

Place the chiles, onion, avocado, cream cheese, and cumin in a blender. Blend at high speed for one minute or until well blended. Serve with tortilla chips.

Pico de Gallo

This recipe makes a great salsa. If you mix it into sour cream, it's also a great topping for fajitas and burgers.

> 4 medium-size ripe tomatoes,
>   cored, seeded, and finely diced
> 1/4 cup minced red onion
> 3 Hatch green chiles, roasted, peeled,
>   stemmed, seeded, and chopped
> 1/2 cup chopped cilantro
> 2 T. fresh lime juice
> 1/4 tsp. salt
> 1/4 tsp. black pepper
> Tortilla chips

Combine the tomatoes, onion, chiles, cilantro, lime juice, salt, and pepper in a medium-size bowl.

Marinate for 30 minutes to blend the flavors.

Serve with tortilla chips.

Great Guacamole

This is my favorite guacamole, made even better with the addition of Hatch chiles.

> 4 ripe avocados, peeled and pitted
> 1 small tomato, peeled, seeded, diced, and drained
> 2 Hatch green chiles, roasted, peeled, stemmed, seeded, and chopped
> 1/4 cup finely diced onion
> 1 tsp. garlic salt
> 1 tsp. ground cumin
> 1 tsp. fajita seasoning
> Juice of 1/2 lime
> Salt, to taste

Scoop out the avocado pulp with a spoon and place it in a medium-size bowl. Mash the pulp with a fork so that the mixture is a bit chunky.

Mix in the tomato, chiles, onion, garlic salt, cumin, fajita seasoning, and lime juice.

For **Cheesy Guacamole**, *add one cup finely shredded Colby Jack cheese and substitute two green onions, finely chopped, for the diced onion.*

Nachos Grande

This is perfect at parties to feed a crowd.

1 pound lean ground beef
1 large onion, chopped
2 Hatch green chiles, roasted, peeled,
    stemmed, seeded, and chopped
1 tsp. seasoned salt
1/2 tsp. ground cumin
2 (16 oz.) cans refried beans
1 (1.25 oz.) package taco seasoning mix
2 cups shredded Monterey Jack cheese
1 cup shredded Cheddar cheese
3/4 cup chunky picante sauce
White tortilla chips
1/2 cup sliced black olives
1 cup guacamole
1/2 cup sour cream
1/4 cup chopped green onion
1 large tomato, diced

Preheat the oven to 400 degrees.

Brown the ground beef with the onion and chiles in a 12-inch skillet over medium heat. Season with the seasoned salt and cumin while the meat is cooking.

Combine the beans, taco seasoning, and Monterey Jack cheese in a medium-size bowl. Spread the bean mixture on the bottom of a 13 x 9 glass baking dish. Cover with the meat mixture. Top with the Cheddar cheese and picante sauce. Bake for 20 to 25 minutes or until thoroughly heated.

Arrange the chips on a serving platter. Spoon the mixture over the chips. Sprinkle with the olives, guacamole, sour cream, onion, and tomato.

Chile Con Queso

A hot cheese dip, loaded with freshly roasted Hatch green chiles and served with tortilla chips for dipping.

    1 cup shredded Monterey Jack cheese
    1/2 cup shredded sharp Cheddar cheese
    3/4 cup half-and-half
    1 medium tomato, seeded and chopped
    3 Hatch green chiles, roasted, peeled,
        stemmed, seeded, and chopped
    2 garlic cloves, minced
    1/4 cup sour cream
    Tortilla chips

Melt the Monterey Jack and Cheddar cheeses in a medium-size saucepan over low heat, stirring often.

Add the cream, stirring constantly to prevent scorching.

Stir in the tomato, chiles, and garlic.

Add the sour cream and stir to mix. Heat through.

Spoon the queso into a serving bowl. Serve with tortilla chips.

 This dip is also great served over grilled chicken breasts, any kind of veggies, for cheese toast with tomato slices, for scalloped cheese potatoes, and as a sauce for mac 'n' cheese.

Meaty Nachos

A quick and easy recipe for a snack or a light lunch.

1 pound lean ground beef
2 Hatch green chiles, roasted, peeled,
   stemmed, seeded, and chopped
1 (16 oz.) can refried beans
White tortilla chips
8 dashes Tabasco sauce
1 cup shredded Cheddar cheese

Brown the ground beef with the chiles in a 12-inch skillet over medium-high heat.

Mix in the refried beans and heat through.

Arrange the chips on a plate. Spoon the meat and bean mixture over the chips. Sprinkle the Tabasco sauce over, then sprinkle with the cheese.

Microwave just until the cheese melts.

Add chopped tomatoes, green onions, and/or black olives. Serve with sour cream and/or guacamole on the side.

Breakfast

Huevos Rancheros

Huevos Rancheros are ranch-style eggs with sauce. Some Hatch in your Huevos is a great way to start the day.

2 cups chopped tomatoes
4 T. butter, divided
1/4 cup finely chopped onion
2 Hatch green chiles, roasted, peeled,
   stemmed, seeded, and chopped
1 garlic clove, minced
Salt, to taste
6 (6-inch) corn tortillas
6 large eggs
Salt and freshly ground black pepper

Put the tomatoes in a food processor or a blender and process until almost smooth. Set aside.

Melt half the butter in a 12-inch skillet over medium heat. Add the onion, chiles, and garlic. Sauté until the onion is tender.

Add the tomatoes and heat to boiling. Cook over medium heat, stirring occasionally, for 5 minutes or until the mixture thickens. Season with salt to taste.

While this is cooking, spray both sides of the tortillas with nonstick cooking spray. Cook in a separate 12-inch skillet over medium heat until browned on both sides, about one minute on each side. Place on serving plates and set aside.

Melt the remaining butter in the skillet. Add the eggs and cook sunny-side up or over easy. Season with salt and pepper to taste.

Place one egg on top of each tortilla and spoon the sauce over.

Hatch Huevos

Can you multi-task first thing in the morning by doing three things at once? Just a few ingredients, ten minutes of your time, and breakfast is ready.

6 Hatch green chiles, roasted, peeled,
   stemmed, seeded, and chopped
4 T. butter, divided
1 small onion, chopped
2 garlic cloves, minced
Salt and freshly ground black pepper
8 medium eggs
8 (6-inch) corn tortillas
1 cup refried beans
1/3 cup chopped cilantro

Place the chiles in a blender and purée until smooth. Set aside.

Melt 2 T. of the butter in a 12-inch skillet over medium heat. Add the onion and sauté until tender. Add the garlic and sauté for one more minute.

Stir in the chile purée, then reduce the heat and simmer for 5 minutes, stirring occasionally. Season with salt and pepper to taste.

While this is cooking, melt the remaining butter in a separate 12-inch skillet over medium-high heat. Add the eggs, four at a time, and cook over easy. Add additional butter if necessary to cook the remaining eggs.

While the eggs are cooking, toast the tortillas in a dry comal or skillet until lightly brown and firm.

Place the beans in a bowl and warm them in the microwave.

Place two tortillas on each plate. Spread equal amounts of the beans and the chile purée over the tortillas, then top with two eggs. Sprinkle with cilantro. Repeat with the remaining tortillas and eggs.

Ham 'n' Eggs

This is a Denver omelet, Hatch chile style. Serve with a side of hash browns.

2 T. butter
2 Hatch green chiles, roasted, peeled,
    stemmed, seeded, and chopped
1/4 cup chopped onion
1/4 cup chopped green bell pepper
1/4 cup chopped pimientos
6 large eggs
1/4 cup milk
1 cup cubed ham
1/4 cup shredded Cheddar cheese, divided
1 Roma tomato, chopped

Melt the butter in a 12-inch skillet over medium heat. Add the chiles, onion, bell pepper, and pimientos. Sauté until the vegetables are tender.

While this is cooking, beat the eggs with the milk in a medium-size bowl. Add the ham. Pour the egg mixture into the skillet. Cook until the sides and center are set, then flip the omelet over. Sprinkle half the cheese on top.

Cook on the second side until lightly browned, then fold the omelet in half. Sprinkle with the remaining cheese and cook for one more minute or until the cheese melts. Sprinkle the tomato over the top.

 If your omelet doesn't stay together when you flip it, you have two choices: Decide you want scrambled eggs or use two separate skillets to make smaller omelets. Either way, this breakfast is delicious.

Easy Salsa Omelet

This omelet serves one and is a quick and easy breakfast. If you'd prefer a breakfast taco, scramble it and wrap it in a warm flour tortilla.

1 T. butter
1 T. Hatch green chiles, roasted, peeled,
   stemmed, seeded, and chopped
1/2 T. finely chopped onion
1 large egg
1 T. milk
1/4 cup shredded Cheddar cheese, divided
4 T. chunky salsa
1 cilantro sprig

Melt the butter in an 8-inch skillet over medium heat. Add the chiles and onion. Sauté until the onion is tender.

While this is cooking, beat the egg with the milk in a small bowl. Pour the egg mixture into the skillet. Cook until the sides and center are set, then flip the omelet over. Sprinkle half the cheese on top.

Cook on the second side until lightly browned, then fold the omelet in half. Remove to a plate.

Add the salsa to the skillet and stir to heat it.

Top the omelet with the salsa. Sprinkle with the remaining cheese. Garnish with a cilantro sprig.

Hatch, New Mexico, is where the Hatch happens. Hatch chiles are harvested in late July and brought to market.

Eggs Olé

This breakfast is a bright beginning for any day. Serve the eggs alone or wrap them in a warm flour tortilla and top with salsa for a breakfast taco.

2 T. butter
3 T. diced onion
3 T. diced green bell pepper
1 small garlic clove, minced
4 T. Hatch green chiles, roasted, peeled, stemmed, seeded, and chopped
1 Roma tomato, chopped
1/4 tsp. chili powder
2 large eggs
2 T. milk
Salt and freshly ground black pepper
2 T. chopped cilantro

Melt the butter in a 10-inch skillet over medium heat. Add the onion and bell pepper. Sauté until the onion and bell pepper are tender.

Reduce the heat to medium-low. Add the garlic, chiles, tomato, and chili powder. Cook for 2 more minutes, stirring occasionally.

While this is cooking, beat the eggs with the milk in a small bowl.

Pour the egg mixture into the skillet and stir to scramble. Season with salt and pepper to taste. Garnish with cilantro.

 *To make **Cheesy Eggs Olé**, top with a handful of shredded Cheddar cheese.*

Green Chile Scramble

Serve this with a side of bacon or sausage. Some green chile salsa is also good on the side.

8 large eggs
1/4 cup milk
1/4 cup minced onion
2 Hatch green chiles, roasted, peeled,
   stemmed, seeded, and chopped
1/8 tsp. ground cumin
1/8 tsp. garlic powder
Salt and freshly ground black pepper
3 T. butter
1/2 cup shredded Colby Jack cheese
Flour tortillas, warmed

Beat the eggs with the milk in a medium-size bowl.

Stir in the onion, chiles, cumin, and garlic powder. Season with salt and pepper to taste.

Melt the butter in a 12-inch skillet over medium heat. Add the egg mixture and stir to scramble. Top with the cheese and cook for one more minute or until the cheese melts.

Serve with warm flour tortillas.

Breakfast Burritos

Serve this with salsa and/or sour cream.

8 large eggs
1/4 cup milk
2 Hatch green chiles, roasted, peeled,
    stemmed, seeded, and chopped
1/2 pound crumbled chorizo sausage
1 (16 oz.) can refried beans
4 (10-inch) flour tortillas, warmed
1/2 cup shredded Colby Jack cheese

Beat the eggs with the milk in a medium-size bowl. Stir in the chiles. Set aside.

Heat a 12-inch skillet over medium-high heat. Add the chorizo. Cook for 5 minutes or until cooked through. Drain.

Reduce the heat to medium. Add the egg mixture and stir to scramble.

While this is cooking, place the beans in a small bowl and warm them in the microwave.

Spread the beans on the tortillas. Top with the scrambled eggs and cheese. Fold in the sides and roll up. Repeat with the remaining tortillas.

Green Chile Hash and Eggs

A bed of Hatch chiles and crispy potatoes are the perfect complement for your eggs in the morning.

4 T. butter, divided
1-1/2 cups Hatch green chiles, roasted,
    peeled, stemmed, seeded, and chopped
1/2 cup chopped onion
2 cups cubed, peeled, cooked potatoes
Salt and freshly ground black pepper
4 large eggs
1/2 cup salsa, warmed

Melt half the butter in a 12-inch skillet over medium heat. Add the chiles and onion. Sauté until the onion is tender.

Add the potatoes and cook for 5 minutes or until the potatoes are browned, stirring once or twice. Season with salt and pepper to taste.

While this is cooking, melt the remaining butter in a separate 12-inch skillet over medium-high heat and cook the eggs sunny-side up or over easy.

Place the chile-potato mixture on individual plates and top with an egg. Serve with salsa.

Ham and Cheese Huevos

Poached eggs nestled on a bed of ham, mushrooms, garlic, onion, and chiles, topped with cheese.

1 T. butter
1/4 pound smoked ham, diced
1 (8 oz.) container sliced mushrooms, chopped
1 cup Hatch green chiles, roasted,
   peeled, stemmed, seeded, and chopped
1 garlic clove, minced
1 (8 oz.) container sour cream
2 T. chopped cilantro
6 large eggs
Salt and freshly ground black pepper
3/4 cup shredded Cheddar cheese

Preheat the oven to 350 degrees. Lightly spray a one-quart glass casserole with nonstick cooking spray. Set aside.

Melt the butter in a 12-inch skillet over medium-high heat. Add the ham and mushrooms. Sauté for 2 minutes, then add the chiles and garlic. Sauté for one more minute

Remove the skillet from the heat and stir in the sour cream and cilantro, then spoon the mixture into the prepared baking dish. With the back of a spoon, make six rounded hollows in the mixture. Break an egg into each hollow. Season with salt and pepper to taste. Bake for 20 minutes or until the egg whites are set.

Remove from the oven and sprinkle the cheese over the top. Return to the oven and bake for 5 to 10 more minutes or until the cheese is melted and the egg yolks are set.

 Buy the smoked ham from the deli or use any kind of cooked or baked ham.

Chile Omelet

This breakfast will open your eyes and get you going in the morning.

> 4 T. butter, divided
> 1/2 cup diced tomato
> 3 T. chopped onion
> 2 Hatch green chiles, roasted, peeled,
>   stemmed, seeded, and chopped
> 2 large eggs
> 2 T. milk
> 1/4 cup shredded Monterey Jack cheese
> 1 tsp. chopped cilantro

Melt half the butter in an 8-inch skillet over medium heat. Add the tomato, onion, and chiles. Cook for 3 minutes or until the onion is tender. Remove and set aside in a small bowl.

While this is cooking, beat the eggs with the milk in a small bowl.

Melt the remaining butter in the skillet over medium heat. Add the egg mixture and cook until the sides and center are set, then flip the omelet over. Sprinkle the cheese over the top. Cook on the second side until lightly browned, then fold the omelet in half.

Spoon the tomato-onion mixture over the top. Garnish with cilantro.

Serve with a side of sausage. If you're lucky enough to attend a Hatch chile festival, where Hatch chiles are put into almost everything, you can use Hatch chile sausage instead of pork sausage.

Avocado Eggs

The creamy goodness of avocado mixed in with chiles and scrambled eggs lends a whole new definition to creamy eggs.

2 avocados, peeled, pitted, and chopped
1 T. fresh lemon juice
6 large eggs
4 T. milk
4 T. butter
1/4 cup chopped onion
4 Hatch green chiles, roasted, peeled,
    stemmed, seeded, and chopped
Salt and freshly ground black pepper

Place the chopped avocados in a small bowl. Sprinkle the lemon juice over. Set aside.

Beat the eggs with the milk in a medium-size bowl. Set aside.

Melt the butter in a 12-inch skillet over medium heat. Add the onion and sauté until tender.

Add the chiles and sauté for one more minute.

Add the avocados and cook for 2 more minutes.

Pour the egg mixture into the skillet and stir to scramble. Season with salt and pepper to taste.

Green Chile Breakfast Tacos

Spice up your morning with a bit of Hatch chile and salsa.

2 T. vegetable oil
1 cup frozen hash browns, thawed
1 small onion, minced
1 small green bell pepper, minced
4 large eggs
3 T. milk
2 Hatch green chiles, roasted, peeled,
    stemmed, seeded, and chopped
8 (8-inch) flour tortillas, warmed
Salsa, warmed

Heat the oil in a 12-inch skillet over medium-high to high heat. Add the hash browns, onion, and bell pepper. Cook, stirring occasionally, until the hash browns are cooked and the vegetables are tender.

While this is cooking, beat the eggs with the milk and chiles in a small bowl.

Push the hash brown mixture to the side of the skillet. Pour in the egg mixture and stir to scramble, then mix the eggs with the hash brown mixture.

Spoon into tortillas and fold in half. Serve with salsa.

Quiche

Perfect for a Sunday brunch or for breakfast any other day of the week.

> 1 (9-inch) unbaked pie shell
> 4 medium eggs
> 1 tsp. salt
> 1/2 tsp. ground cumin
> 1/2 cup chopped onion
> 1 tsp. chili powder
> 1 tsp. black pepper
> 1 cup Hatch green chiles, roasted, peeled,
> stemmed, seeded, and chopped
> 2 cups half-and-half
> 1 cup shredded Monterey Jack cheese
> 8 slices bacon, crisp-cooked and crumbled

Preheat the oven to 425 degrees. Place the crust in a 9-inch pie pan and set aside.

Separate the egg yolks from the whites. Beat the egg yolks in a medium-size bowl. Whip the egg whites until thick and foamy in a separate medium-size bowl. Fold the egg whites into the yolks, then mix in the salt, cumin, onion, chili powder, pepper, and chiles.

Add the half-and-half to the mixture and blend well.

Sprinkle the cheese over the bottom of the pie crust, then pour the egg mixture over the cheese.

Sprinkle the crumbled bacon over the top. Bake for 25 to 30 minutes or until browned and firm.

 This is even better served with browned sausage links and a green chile sauce.

Sausage and Egg Casserole

This takes an hour to cook, so make it the night before and refrigerate it, then pop it into the oven first thing in the morning.

1 pound pork sausage, crumbled
8 medium eggs
3 cups half-and-half
12 (8-inch) flour tortillas
4 Hatch green chiles, roasted, peeled,
  stemmed, seeded, and chopped
1/2 cup frozen corn, thawed
2 cups shredded Monterey Jack cheese, divided
2 T. chili powder
1 medium tomato, chopped
1/2 cup chopped green onion

Lightly spray a 13 x 9 glass baking dish with nonstick cooking spray. Set aside.

Cook the sausage in a 12-inch skillet over medium-high heat. Drain and set aside.

Beat the eggs with the half-and-half in a large bowl.

Lightly dip each tortilla in the egg mixture. Lay three tortillas on the bottom of the prepared baking dish, overlapping as needed. Layer one-third each of the sausage, chiles, corn, and 1-1/2 cups of the cheese. Sprinkle with one-third of the chili powder. Repeat the layers, ending with tortillas. Pour the remaining egg mixture over. Sprinkle the remaining cheese over the top. Cover and refrigerate overnight.

When ready to cook, preheat the oven to 400 degrees and bring the casserole to room temperature. Cover with aluminum foil and bake for 35 minutes. Remove from the oven and uncover. Return to the oven and bake for 10 more minutes to brown the top.

Sprinkle the tomato and onion on top.

Breakfast Casserole

This breakfast has it all—potatoes, cheese, onion, chiles, ham, and eggs.

　　1 cup melted butter, divided
　　1 medium onion, diced
　　5 Hatch green chiles, roasted, peeled,
　　　　stemmed, seeded, and chopped
　　1 (32 oz.) package frozen shredded
　　　　hash browns, thawed
　　2 cups diced ham
　　6 large eggs
　　1 cup evaporated milk
　　2 cups shredded Monterey Jack cheese
　　2 cups shredded Cheddar cheese
　　Salt and freshly ground black pepper

Preheat the oven to 425 degrees. Lightly spray a 13 x 9 glass baking dish with nonstick cooking spray. Set aside.

Heat 2 T. of the butter in a 12-inch skillet over medium heat. Add the onion and sauté until tender. Add the chiles and sauté for one more minute.

Add the hash browns and mix with the onion-chile mixture. Place this mixture in the prepared baking dish.

Pour the remaining melted butter over the hash brown mixture. Bake for 20 minutes. Remove from the oven and sprinkle the ham over the hash browns.

Beat the eggs with the milk in a medium-size bowl. Pour over the ham and hash browns. Top with the Monterey Jack and Cheddar cheeses. Return to the oven and bake for 30 more minutes or until the cheese is melted and lightly brown. Season with salt and pepper to taste.

Breakfast Bundt Cake

Flavored with cinnamon and chiles, all this apple cake needs is a cup of morning coffee to complement it.

Flour, for the baking dish
3 cups all-purpose flour
1 T. ground cinnamon
1/2 tsp. ground nutmeg
1/2 tsp. ground allspice
1/8 tsp. ground cloves
1 tsp. baking soda
1/4 tsp. salt
1-1/4 cups canola oil
1-3/4 cups granulated sugar
3 medium eggs
1 T. vanilla extract
1 cup Hatch chiles, roasted, peeled,
    stemmed, seeded, and chopped
3 large apples, peeled, cored, and diced

Preheat the oven to 350 degrees. Lightly spray a 10-inch bundt pan with nonstick cooking spray. Dust with flour and set aside.

Combine the flour, cinnamon, nutmeg, allspice, cloves, baking soda, and salt in a medium-size bowl. Set aside.

Beat the oil and sugar together until combined in a large bowl. Add the eggs, one at a time, and beat well.

Stir in the vanilla and half the flour mixture. Stir in the chiles, apples, and the remaining flour mixture. Spoon the batter into the prepared baking dish. Bake for one hour and 15 minutes or until a toothpick inserted in the center comes out clean.

Let the cake cool for 10 minutes, then turn it out onto a serving dish.

Salads

Grilled Chicken Strip Salad

This is a great salad to enjoy on a hot summer night when you don't want to turn on the oven to make dinner.

4 cups coarsely chopped mixed salad greens
1 (6 oz.) package pre-cooked Southwest seasoned
   chicken breast strips, cut into bite-size pieces
1 cup shredded Cheddar cheese
2 tomatoes, each cut into 8 wedges
1 avocado, peeled, pitted, and coarsely mashed
1/2 (15 oz.) can black beans, drained and rinsed
2 Hatch green chiles, roasted, peeled,
   stemmed, seeded, and chopped
1/2 cup sliced green onion
1/4 cup sliced black olives
1 T. chili powder
2 tsp. garlic powder
Ranch dressing

Place the salad greens in a large serving bowl.

Add the chicken, cheese, tomatoes, avocado, beans, chiles, onion, and olives. Sprinkle with chili powder and garlic powder. Toss to mix.

Serve the dressing on the side.

 *Crush tortilla chips or Doritos and sprinkle them on top of the salad. To make a **Grilled Chicken Wrap**, wrap individual portions of all of the ingredients in warmed flour tortillas. Substitute salsa instead of Ranch dressing. To make a **Chicken Pasta Salad**, add cooked pasta and corn. Serve with Italian or balsamic dressing.*

Black Bean Pasta Salad

You can use any type pasta in this salad.

1 cup elbow macaroni
1/2 cup mayonnaise
1/2 cup plain yogurt
3 T. fresh lime juice
1 tsp. ground cumin
1/2 tsp. salt
1/4 tsp. black pepper
1 small green bell pepper, chopped
1 small red bell pepper, chopped
1/2 cup chopped green onion
4 Hatch green chiles, roasted, peeled,
   stemmed, seeded, and chopped
1 (15 oz.) can black beans, drained and rinsed
1/2 cup frozen corn, thawed
2 T. chopped cilantro

Cook the pasta according to the package directions. Drain in a colander and rinse with cold water. Set aside.

Combine the mayonnaise, yogurt, lime juice, cumin, salt, and pepper in a medium-size serving bowl.

Add the pasta and stir to coat.

Stir in the green and red bell peppers, onion, chiles, beans, corn, and cilantro.

The heat of the chiles is concentrated in the central part of the pod, which produces the seeds. The heat comes from capsaicin.

Perfect Pasta Salad

Pasta, chiles, tomatoes, and cheese, tossed with a green chile vinaigrette. The vinaigrette is perfect on the pasta salad and is also a great dressing for any other salad.

4 cups cooked pasta, rinsed and cooled
1 large tomato, chopped
1 avocado, peeled, pitted, and chopped
2 Hatch green chiles, roasted, peeled, stemmed, seeded, and chopped
1/2 cup diced Cheddar cheese
1/4 cup finely chopped red onion
Green Chile Vinaigrette (recipe follows)
Tortilla chips

Combine the pasta, tomato, avocado, chiles, cheese, and onion in a large serving bowl. Toss with the vinaigrette and serve with tortilla chips.

Green Chile Vinaigrette

1/4 cup olive oil, divided
2 garlic cloves, minced
2 Hatch green chiles, roasted, peeled, stemmed, seeded, and minced
2 T. cider vinegar
2 T. fresh lime juice
Salt and freshly ground black pepper

Heat 1 T. of the oil in a 12-inch skillet over medium heat. Add the garlic and chiles. Sauté for one minute.

Place in a blender, along with the remaining oil, vinegar, and lime juice. Blend until smooth. Season with salt and pepper to taste.

Chicken Salsa Salad

Salsa and chicken are a great combination. They're even better when the chicken is southwest seasoned and the salad has chopped Hatch chiles. This salad also makes a nice wrap for lunch, served in a warm flour tortilla.

4 tsp. taco seasoning
3 skinless, boneless chicken breasts
2 to 3 T. vegetable oil
2 Hatch green chiles, roasted, peeled,
    stemmed, seeded, and chopped
1 red bell pepper, chopped
1 avocado, peeled, pitted, and sliced
2 T. fresh lime juice
1 head romaine lettuce, chopped
1 (8 oz.) jar salsa
1 large tomato, chopped

Place the taco seasoning on a plate. Dredge the chicken in the taco seasoning.

Heat the oil in a 12-inch skillet over medium-high heat. Add the chicken and brown it on both sides. Remove to a cutting board and cut into cubes. Set aside to cool.

Add the chiles and bell pepper to the skillet, adding more oil if necessary. Cook until the bell pepper is tender. Remove and set aside.

Place the avocado slices in a small bowl. Sprinkle them with the lime juice.

Place the lettuce in a large serving bowl or on a platter. Toss with salsa, then place the chiles, bell pepper, avocado, and tomato over the lettuce. Top with chicken.

Taco Salad

This can be a salad or a wrap. If you'd prefer a wrap, use four (8-inch) flour tortillas, warmed in the microwave. Use only one cup chopped lettuce. Place all the ingredients in the tortilla and wrap.

1 pound lean ground beef
1 (1.25 oz.) package taco seasoning mix
1/2 cup water
2 Hatch green chiles, roasted, peeled,
    stemmed, seeded, and chopped
White tortilla chips
6 cups lettuce, cut into ribbons
1/2 cup shredded Cheddar cheese
1/2 cup shredded Monterey Jack cheese
1 (8 oz.) container sour cream
1 avocado, peeled, pitted, and mashed
1 medium tomato, chopped

Brown the ground beef in a 12-inch skillet over medium heat. Stir in the taco seasoning, water, and chiles. Bring to a boil, then reduce the heat and simmer for 10 minutes, stirring occasionally.

While this is cooking, preheat the oven to 200 degrees. Spread the tortilla chips on a baking sheet and warm them in the oven for 5 minutes.

Mix the lettuce and tortilla chips together on individual plates. Spoon the meat mixture over. Top with the Cheddar and Monterey Jack cheeses, sour cream, avocado, and tomato.

 *To make **Taco Chicken Salad**, use 2 cups chopped, shredded chicken instead of the ground beef. Add 1/4 cup sliced black olives and 1/2 cup dark red kidney beans, drained and rinsed.*

Chicken Tostada Salad

No bowl or utensil needed.

2 cups shredded, cooked chicken
4 green onions, chopped
3 Hatch green chiles, roasted, peeled,
    stemmed, seeded, and chopped
4 cups chopped iceberg lettuce
1 large tomato, seeded and diced
1/2 cup shredded Mexican Blend cheese
1/4 cup red wine vinegar
3/4 cup olive oil
Salt and freshly ground black pepper
1 cup refried beans
12 (6-inch) tostadas
8 T. sour cream
2 avocados, peeled, pitted, and thinly sliced

Combine the chicken, onions, and chiles, in a medium-size bowl. Set aside. Combine the lettuce, tomato, and cheese in a separate medium-size bowl. Set aside. Whisk the vinegar, oil, and the salt and pepper to taste in a small bowl. Set aside.

Put the beans in a small bowl and warm in the microwave. Spread a layer of beans on each tostada. Spoon the sour cream over. Top with the avocado slices.

Pour enough of the dressing on the chicken mixture to coat it generously, then toss well. Scatter the chicken mixture over the avocado slices. Toss the remaining dressing with the lettuce mixture, then sprinkle the lettuce over the chicken mixture.

 If you can't find tostadas, substitute 12 (6-inch) corn tortillas. Fry them in vegetable oil until crisp, then drain on paper towels.

Chile Chicken Salad

Enjoy with crackers or tortilla chips for a salad, or make a sandwich with whole wheat bread.

2 cups diced, cooked chicken
1 cup Hatch green chiles, roasted, peeled, stemmed, seeded, and chopped
1 green onion, chopped
1/2 cup diced celery
1/2 cup mayonnaise
1/4 cup Ranch dressing
3 to 4 Romaine lettuce leaves
Whole wheat crackers or tortilla chips

Combine the chicken, chiles, onion, and celery in a medium-size bowl.

Add the mayonnaise and dressing. Toss to mix.

Serve on a bed of lettuce with crackers or chips.

 To make **Toasty Chicken Chile Sandwich,** *toast 1/4 cup chopped almonds in a dry skillet. Omit the Ranch dressing and increase the mayonnaise to 1/4 cup. Add a small handful of seedless green grapes, cut in half. Serve on whole wheat bread.*

Chicken Fajita Salad

These fajitas are served on a bed of lettuce instead of wrapped in a tortilla.

  1 T. vegetable oil
  2 green onions, chopped
  1/2 tsp. crushed red pepper flakes
  1 (6 oz.) package pre-cooked Southwest seasoned
    chicken breast strips, cut into bite-size pieces
  2 Hatch green chiles, roasted, peeled,
    stemmed, seeded, and chopped
  1 head iceberg lettuce, chopped
  2 medium tomatoes, chopped
  2 avocados, peeled, pitted, and chopped
  3/4 cup salsa
  1/2 cup sour cream

Heat the oil in a 12-inch skillet over medium heat. Add the onions and red pepper flakes. Sauté until the onions are tender.

Stir in the chicken and chiles. Heat through.

Place the lettuce on individual plates. Top with the chicken mixture, then sprinkle with the tomatoes and avocados. Top with a spoonful or two of the salsa and a dollop of sour cream.

Everyday Salad

*I eat this salad almost every day before dinner. Sometimes it **is** dinner when I add pasta, chicken, black beans, and corn.*

4 cups ripped Romaine lettuce leaves
1 (15.5 oz.) can dark red kidney beans,
   drained and rinsed
1/4 cup minced onion
2 Hatch green chiles, roasted, peeled,
   stemmed, seeded, and chopped
2 medium tomatoes, chopped
1 small cucumber, sliced
6 slices bacon, crisp-cooked and crumbled
1 (8 oz.) package shredded Mexican blend cheese
Ranch dressing, to taste
Freshly ground black pepper, to taste

Place the lettuce, beans, onion, chiles, tomatoes, cucumber, bacon, and cheese in a large serving bowl. Add the dressing and toss to mix. Season with pepper to taste.

 *To make an **Everyday Chicken-Pasta Salad**, add cooked, chopped chicken, corn, black beans, and cooked, drained, and cooled pasta.*

Enchilada Salad

Shredded chicken encased in a chile-garlic-tomato-sauced corn tortilla and topped with lettuce, avocado, and cheese.

1 skinless, boneless chicken breast
1/2 small onion, chopped
4 garlic cloves, peeled, divided
1 T. minced cilantro
1/4 tsp. dried oregano
3 Hatch green chiles, roasted, peeled,
    stemmed, seeded, and chopped
3 medium ripe tomatoes, chopped
2 T. vegetable oil
8 (6-inch) corn tortillas
1 cup shredded lettuce
1 avocado, peeled, pitted, and coarsely chopped
1/2 cup shredded Monterey Jack cheese
1/2 cup sour cream

Place the chicken, onion, two garlic cloves, the cilantro, and oregano in a large saucepan. Cover with water, bring to a boil, then reduce the heat and simmer for 15 minutes or until the chicken is cooked through. Remove the chicken to a cutting board. Let cool slightly, then shred it with two forks. Set aside. Remove the onion and garlic to a small bowl. Mash the onion and garlic. Set aside.

Place the chiles, tomatoes, and remaining garlic in a blender. Process until the consistency is a smooth paste. Spoon the sauce into a shallow bowl, large enough to hold the tortillas.

Heat the oil in a 12-inch skillet over medium heat.

Dip a tortilla in the chile-tomato sauce, then place it in the skillet and soften it, turning once, for about 10 seconds per side. Remove it to a plate. Repeat with the remaining tortillas, adding more oil if necessary.

Place a spoonful of the shredded chicken in the center of each tortilla. Add a little bit of the onion-garlic mixture. Roll up tightly.

Place two tortillas on a plate. Top with any remaining chile-tomato sauce and the onion-garlic mixture. Garnish with lettuce and avocado. Top with cheese and a dollop of sour cream.

Eating chiles is an experience unto itself. Chile stimulates the appetite, dilates blood vessels, and speeds up the metabolism. If you eat enough chiles, you'll also experience watery eyes and a runny nose, along with flushing and sweating in the head area and neck.

Avocado Salad

Clean and crisp, this salad makes a perfect light lunch with tortilla chips or crackers.

2 medium tomatoes, chopped
5 green onions, chopped
3 Hatch green chiles, roasted, peeled, stemmed, seeded, and chopped
2 avocados, peeled, pitted, and chopped
Juice of 1/2 lemon

Combine the tomatoes, onions, chiles, and avocado in a medium-size serving bowl. Toss to mix. Squeeze the lemon juice over.

Steak Salad

This salad is like fajitas in a bowl.

3/4 pound sirloin steak
4 garlic cloves, chopped
Juice of one lime, divided
4 tsp. olive oil, divided
1 T. red wine vinegar
1/2 T. chili powder
1 tsp. ground cumin
1 tsp. paprika
6 cups chopped Romaine lettuce
5 green onions, thinly sliced
1 (8 oz.) can corn, drained and rinsed
3 Hatch green chiles, roasted, peeled,
    stemmed, seeded, and chopped
2 avocados, peeled, pitted, and chopped
2 medium tomatoes, chopped
5 T. chopped cilantro
1 cup lightly crushed tortilla chips

Place the steak in a medium-size bowl with the garlic, half the lime juice, and half the oil. Cover and marinate in the refrigerator for 30 minutes.

Whisk the remaining lime juice and oil with the vinegar, chili powder, cumin, and paprika in a small bowl.

Broil or grill the steak. Transfer to a cutting board and cut into strips. Set aside.

Arrange the lettuce on a serving platter. Toss with the onions. Pour half the dressing over, then arrange the corn, chiles, avocados, and tomatoes over the top. Sprinkle with cilantro. Arrange the steak and tortilla chips on top and pour the rest of the dressing over.

Soups and Stews

Black Bean Potato Soup

The creamy texture of black beans, along with the potatoes and fresh spinach, make this soup special.

3/4 cup chopped onion
2 tsp. minced garlic
1/4 tsp. dried oregano
1-1/2 tsp. ground cumin
1-1/2 cups water
2 beef bouillon cubes
2 small red potatoes, scrubbed and chopped
2 (15 oz.) cans black beans, drained and rinsed
4 to 5 fresh spinach leaves, washed and chopped
2 Hatch green chiles, roasted, peeled,
   stemmed, seeded, and chopped
1 cup crushed Fritos
1 cup shredded Cheddar cheese

Combine the onion, garlic, oregano, cumin, water, bouillon, potatoes, and beans in a large saucepan. Bring to a boil, then reduce the heat, cover, and simmer for 25 minutes, stirring occasionally.

Add the spinach and chiles. Cook for 5 more minutes.

Ladle into individual serving bowls. Sprinkle with the crushed Fritos and cheese.

Black Bean Soup

If you'd prefer a creamier soup, mash about half of the black beans. They'll thicken the broth.

10 slices bacon, chopped
1 red bell pepper, chopped
1 small onion, chopped
3 carrots, chopped
2 garlic cloves, chopped
2 cups chicken broth
1-1/4 cups water
2 (15 oz.) cans black beans, drained and rinsed
2 T. finely chopped cilantro
1 T. fresh lemon juice
1 tsp. dried oregano
1/2 tsp. dried thyme
1/4 tsp. crushed red pepper flakes
4 Hatch green chiles, roasted, peeled,
    stemmed, seeded, and chopped
1/8 tsp. black pepper
Sour cream
1 medium tomato, diced

Cook the bacon with the bell pepper, onion, and carrots in a large saucepan over medium-high heat until the bacon is crisp and the vegetables are tender. Add the garlic and sauté for one more minute. Drain.

Stir in the broth, water, beans, cilantro, lemon juice, oregano, thyme, red pepper flakes, chiles, and pepper. Bring to a boil, then reduce the heat, cover, and simmer for 10 minutes, stirring occasionally.

Ladle into individual soup bowls. Top with a dollop of sour cream and garnish with the diced tomatoes.

Refried Bean Soup

This creamy soup is flavored with Hatch chiles, jalapeño peppers, and bacon.

> 1 (16 oz.) can refried beans
> 2 cups chicken broth
> 1 (15.5 oz.) can pinto beans, drained and rinsed
> 2 Hatch green chiles, roasted, peeled,
>   stemmed, seeded, and chopped
> 2 garlic cloves, minced
> 2 jalapeño peppers, stemmed, seeded, and chopped
> 1/4 tsp. black pepper
> 2 tsp. chili powder
> 6 slices bacon
> 1 bunch green onions, chopped, divided
> 1 green bell pepper, chopped
> 1 (8 oz.) package shredded Cheddar cheese

Whisk the refried beans with the broth in a large saucepan over medium heat.

Stir in the pinto beans, chiles, garlic, jalapeños, pepper, and chili powder. Reduce the heat to low and simmer for 10 minutes, stirring occasionally.

While this is cooking, cook the bacon in a 12-inch skillet over medium heat until crisp. Remove and drain on paper towels. Set aside.

Add 3/4 of the onions and the bell pepper to the skillet. Sauté in the bacon drippings until tender.

Crumble the bacon and add it to the bean mixture. Stir in the onions and bell pepper. Heat through.

Ladle into individual soup bowls. Garnish with the remaining onions and cheese.

Hatch Hoppin' John

Hoppin' John is a traditional New Year's Day soup which is said to bring good luck and fortune.

2 T. olive oil
1 red bell pepper, chopped
1 medium onion, chopped
2 celery stalks, chopped
2 garlic cloves, finely chopped
3 (15 oz.) cans black-eyed peas,
   drained and rinsed
2 Hatch green chiles, roasted, peeled,
   stemmed, seeded, and chopped
2 cups chopped, cooked ham
1 (11 oz.) can tomato juice
1 (14.5 oz.) can diced tomatoes

Heat the oil in a large saucepan over medium heat. Add the bell pepper, onion, and celery. Sauté until tender. Add the garlic and sauté for one more minute.

Add the black-eyed peas, chiles, cooked ham, tomato juice, and tomatoes. Bring to a boil, then reduce the heat, cover, and simmer for 45 minutes, stirring occasionally.

Heat from chiles can prove to be too much to handle. If you experience distress, sour cream served with your meal to cool the palate will give you relief. A glass of cold milk is the best remedy. If you drink water, you'll only be spreading the heat.

Squash Soup

Chayote is a light green, crinkly-ended relative of zucchini. It has a light, fresh flavor and texture.

2 T. butter
4 chayote squash, peeled, seeded,
   and cut into one-half inch cubes
2 medium onions, chopped
1 red bell pepper, chopped
2 garlic cloves, minced
1/4 cup all-purpose flour
4 cups chicken broth
2 cups frozen corn, thawed
2 cups Hatch green chiles, roasted, peeled,
   stemmed, seeded, and chopped
2 cups milk
1-1/2 tsp. salt
1 tsp. ground cumin
1/2 tsp. chili powder
2 T. fresh lime juice
1/4 cup shredded Cheddar cheese
6 slices bacon, crisp-cooked and crumbled

Melt the butter in a large saucepan over medium-high heat. Add the squash, onions, and bell pepper. Sauté until the vegetables are tender. Add the garlic and sauté for one more minute. Add the flour and cook, stirring, for 2 minutes.

Add the broth, corn, chiles, milk, salt, cumin, and chili powder. Stir until all the flour has been incorporated. Bring to a boil, stirring, then reduce the heat and simmer for 45 minutes, stirring occasionally.

Ladle into individual soup bowls. Squirt some lime juice into each bowl. Garnish with cheese and bacon.

Gazpacho

Very cool and refreshing with just the right amount of kick from the chiles.

3 medium tomatoes, chopped
1 medium cucumber, peeled and chopped
1 green bell pepper, chopped
3 green onions, chopped
2-1/2 cups tomato juice
1 cup Hatch green chiles, roasted, peeled,
    stemmed, seeded, and chopped
2 T. white wine
1/4 tsp. celery salt
1/2 tsp. black pepper
1/2 tsp. garlic salt
Juice of one lime
1/4 cup chopped cilantro

Mix the tomatoes, cucumber, bell pepper, onions, tomato juice, chiles, wine, celery salt, pepper, garlic salt, and lime juice in a large bowl. Chill in the refrigerator for 2 hours, stirring occasionally.

Ladle into individual soup bowls. Garnish with cilantro.

Chicken Chiles 'n' Corn Soup

This delicious soup, simmering on the stovetop, will fill your home with a wonderful aroma.

3 T. cornstarch
3 T. cold water
4 cups chopped chicken
1 (15 oz.) can white shoepeg corn
2 (14 oz.) cans chicken broth
1 (8 oz.) can tomato sauce
2 (14.5 oz.) cans diced tomatoes
4 Hatch green chiles, roasted, peeled,
   stemmed, seeded, and chopped
1 medium onion, chopped
1 tsp. garlic powder
1 tsp. dried oregano

Mix the cornstarch with the water in a small bowl until it forms a smooth paste. This will thicken the soup as it cooks.

Place all the ingredients in a large saucepan. Stir to mix. Bring to a boil, then reduce the heat, cover, and simmer for 2 hours, stirring occasionally.

 To make **Creamy Chicken, Chiles, 'n' Corn Cheesy Soup,** *use half-and-half instead of the chicken broth. Add one cup shredded Monterey Jack cheese during the last five minutes of cooking.*

Chicken Pinto Soup

Soak the beans the night before. If you plan to have this for dinner instead of lunch, cook it on low heat in a crock pot for 7 hours.

> 2 (16 oz.) packages dried pinto beans
> 2 T. olive oil
> 3 skinless, boneless chicken breasts, chopped
> 2 (14.5 oz.) cans Mexican style tomatoes
> 1 (15 oz.) can whole kernel corn, drained
> 2 (1.25 oz.) packages taco seasoning mix
> 1/2 cup fresh lemon juice
> 3 Hatch green chiles, roasted, peeled,
>   stemmed, seeded, and chopped
> 1 medium onion, chopped
> Sour cream

Rinse the beans and soak them in a large bowl of cold water overnight. Drain in a colander, rinse under cold running water, and drain again. Set aside.

Heat the oil in a large saucepan over medium-high heat. Add the chicken and brown it on all sides.

Add the beans to the cooked chicken. Cover with water.

Add the tomatoes, corn, taco seasoning, lemon juice, chiles, and onion. Bring to a boil, then reduce the heat and simmer for one hour or until the beans are tender, stirring occasionally.

Ladle into individual soup bowls. Top with a dollop of sour cream.

 Top this with a sprinkling of chopped green onion and crushed tortilla chips for crunchiness.

Hominy Soup

Hominy is corn (maize) which has been soaked in an alkali solution of lime to remove the hull and germ, causing the corn to puff up to twice its size.

4 skinless, boneless chicken breasts
1 (14.5 oz.) can diced tomatoes
2 garlic cloves, minced
1 tsp. ground cumin
1 medium onion, coarsely chopped
6 Hatch green chiles, roasted, peeled,
   stemmed, seeded, and chopped
1 (15.5 oz.) can hominy, drained and rinsed
Salt and freshly ground black pepper
1 lime, cut in half
1/4 cup chopped cilantro

Place the chicken in a large saucepan and cover with water. Bring to a boil, then reduce the heat and simmer for 15 minutes or until the chicken is cooked through. Remove the chicken to a cutting board and cut into strips.

Return the chicken to the pan. Add the tomatoes, garlic, cumin, onion, chiles, and hominy. Bring to a boil, then reduce the heat and simmer for 15 minutes, stirring occasionally. Season with salt and pepper to taste.

Ladle into individual soup bowls. Squirt some lime juice into each bowl. Garnish with cilantro.

 Squirting fresh lime juice into the soup just before serving adds a citrus zing of freshness.

Chicken Tortilla Soup

There are many versions of Tortilla Soup; the constant ingredient is tortilla strips. The strips are usually fried but this recipe cuts the fat by baking them in the oven.

3 skinless, boneless chicken breasts
3-1/2 cups chicken broth
1 T. butter
1 small onion, chopped
1/2 tsp. ground cumin
1 garlic clove, minced
1 (14.5 oz.) can diced tomatoes
1 (8 oz.) can tomato sauce
4 Hatch green chiles, roasted, peeled,
    stemmed, seeded, and chopped
1/4 cup chopped cilantro
1 tsp. dried oregano
6 (6-inch) corn tortillas
1/2 cup shredded Monterey Jack cheese
1/2 cup shredded Cheddar cheese

Place the chicken and broth in a large saucepan. Bring to a boil, then reduce the heat and simmer for 15 minutes or until the chicken is cooked through. Remove the pan from the heat and reserve the broth in the pan. Remove the chicken to a cutting board. Let cool slightly, then shred it with two forks and set aside.

Melt the butter in a 10-inch skillet over medium heat. Add the onion and cumin. Sauté until the onion is tender. Add the garlic and sauté for one more minute.

Stir the onion mixture into the reserved broth in the saucepan. Add the shredded chicken, tomatoes, tomato sauce, chiles, cilantro, and oregano. Bring to a low boil, then reduce the heat, cover, and simmer for 20 minutes, stirring occasionally.

While the soup is cooking, preheat the oven to 350 degrees. Cut the tortillas in half, then cut them crosswise into 1/2-inch wide strips. Lightly spray both sides of the tortilla strips with nonstick cooking spray and place them on a baking sheet. Bake for 4 to 5 minutes or until crisp.

Divide the tortilla strips among the soup bowls. Ladle the soup over the tortilla strips. Top with the Monterey Jack and Cheddar cheeses.

Some people like to put the tortilla strips on top of the soup instead of on the bottom.

Pinto Chicken Soup

Quick and easy. A perfect soup if you're short on time.

1 (15.5 oz.) can pinto beans, drained and rinsed
1 small onion, coarsely chopped
2 cups coarsely chopped, cooked chicken
4 Hatch green chiles, roasted, peeled,
   stemmed, seeded, and coarsely chopped
2 cups chicken broth
2 green onions, chopped

Place the beans, onion, chicken, chiles, and broth in a large saucepan. Bring to a boil, then reduce the heat and simmer for 10 minutes or until heated through, stirring occasionally.

Ladle into individual soup bowls. Top with the onions.

Queso Tortilla Soup

Creamy and cheesy, topped with tortilla strips, green onions, and Monterey Jack cheese.

3 T. butter
1 small white onion, minced
6 Hatch green chiles, roasted, peeled,
    stemmed, seeded, and chopped
2 (14.5 oz.) cans plum tomatoes, chopped
1 (6 oz.) package cream cheese,
    cut into small pieces
1 (14 oz.) can chicken broth
1-1/2 cups half-and-half
4 tsp. fresh lemon juice
1/8 tsp. garlic powder
1/8 tsp. cayenne pepper
1/8 tsp. ground cumin
1/2 tsp. salt
3 cups chopped, cooked chicken
1-1/2 cups crisply fried tortilla strips
1/4 cup green onion, chopped
1-1/2 cups shredded Monterey Jack cheese

Melt the butter in a large saucepan over medium heat. Add the onion and sauté until tender. Add the chiles and tomatoes. Cook for 10 minutes, stirring occasionally.

Reduce the heat to medium-low. Add the cream cheese and stir until melted.

Stir in the broth, half-and-half, lemon juice, garlic powder, cayenne pepper, cumin, salt, and chicken. Heat through, but do not allow the soup to boil.

Ladle into individual soup bowls. Top with the tortilla strips, onion, and cheese.

Bacon-Beef Stew

A classic beef stew, made more delicious by the addition of bacon and Hatch chiles.

1/2 pound sliced bacon, coarsely chopped
3 pounds beef stew cubes
2 medium onions, chopped
1 (16 oz.) package baby carrots
5 stalks celery, coarsely chopped
4 Hatch green chiles, roasted, peeled,
    stemmed, seeded, and chopped
4 garlic cloves, minced
3 cups dry red wine
1 cup beef broth
8 medium red potatoes, scrubbed and quartered
Salt and freshly ground black pepper

Cook the bacon in a large saucepan over medium-high heat until crisp. Remove and drain on paper towels. Set aside.

Add the beef and brown it in batches. Remove to a bowl and set aside.

Add the onions, carrots, and celery to the pan. Sauté until the vegetables are tender.

Add the chiles and garlic. Sauté for one more minute.

Add the wine and broth, stirring to scrape up the browned bits from the bottom of the pan.

Return the bacon and the beef to the pan, along with any accumulated juices from the beef. Bring to a boil, then reduce the heat, cover, and simmer, for 2 to 2-1/2 hours, stirring occasionally.

Add the potatoes and simmer for 20 more minutes or until the potatoes are soft. Season with salt and pepper to taste.

Sausage Stew

Hearty and nourishing.

1 tsp. vegetable oil
2-1/2 pounds link sausage, sliced one-half inch thick
1 medium onion, chopped
6 Hatch green chiles, roasted, peeled,
   stemmed, seeded, and chopped
2 garlic cloves, minced
4 cups vegetable broth
5 medium red potatoes, scrubbed and cut into wedges
5 carrots, sliced
1 (15 oz.) can black beans, drained and rinsed
1/2 tsp. ground cumin
2 tsp. dried oregano
Salt and freshly ground black pepper
1 cup shredded Cheddar cheese
1/4 cup chopped cilantro

Heat the oil in a 12-inch skillet over medium-high heat. Add the sausage and onion. Sauté until the sausage is cooked and the onion is tender. Add the chiles and garlic. Sauté for one more minute.

Place the mixture in a large saucepan. Stir in the vegetable broth, potatoes, carrots, beans, cumin, and oregano. Bring to a boil, then reduce the heat and simmer for 30 minutes, stirring occasionally. Season with salt and pepper to taste.

Ladle into individual soup bowls. Garnish with the cheese and cilantro.

 *To make **Chicken-Sausage Stew**, add 2 skinless, boneless chicken breasts, coarsely chopped. Cook the chicken with the sausage and onion.*

Easy Enchilada Soup

If you prefer your enchiladas in a bowl rather than on a plate, you'll enjoy this soup.

1 pound lean ground beef
1/3 cup chopped onion
1/2 cup chopped red bell pepper
3 Hatch green chiles, roasted, peeled,
   stemmed, seeded, and chopped
1 tsp. chili powder
1/2 tsp. ground cumin
1 (8 oz.) can tomato sauce
1 cup beef broth
6 (6-inch) corn tortillas, cut
   into 1/2-inch pieces
1 cup sour cream
1 cup shredded Cheddar cheese

Brown the ground beef with the onion, bell pepper, and chiles in a large saucepan over medium heat. Season with the chili powder and cumin while the meat is cooking

Stir in the tomato sauce and broth. Bring to a boil, then reduce the heat and simmer for 10 minutes, stirring occasionally.

Remove the pan from the heat. Add the tortilla pieces, sour cream, and cheese. Stir until the cheese is melted.

 *To make **Chicken Enchilada Soup**, use 2 skinless, boneless chicken breasts, coarsely chopped, instead of ground beef. Brown the chicken in 2 tsp. olive oil, with the onion, bell pepper, and seasonings. Add the tomato sauce. Use chicken broth instead of beef broth. Simmer for 10 minutes or until the chicken is cooked through and tender. Follow the remainder of the recipe.*

Lentil-Ham Soup

This recipe takes a while to prepare (soaking the lentils) and simmer on the stove top, but is definitely worth the wait.

2 cups dried lentils
1 quart **Hatch Beef Stock** (page 76)
1 quart bottled beer
5 slices bacon, chopped
1 large onion, chopped
4 Hatch green chiles, roasted, peeled,
    stemmed, seeded, and chopped
2 garlic cloves, minced
1 cup chopped smoked boneless ham
4 carrots, sliced
4 celery stalks, chopped
8 whole peppercorns, cracked
1 bay leaf
1 tsp. grated nutmeg
2 tsp. dried rosemary
Salt and freshly ground black pepper
1/2 cup chopped cilantro

Place the lentils in a large bowl. Add the beef stock and beer. Soak the lentils for 2 hours. Add water if necessary to cover the lentils by 3 inches.

Cook the bacon in a 12-inch skillet over medium-high heat until crisp. Remove and drain on paper towels. Set aside. Add the onion to the skillet. Sauté until the onion is tender. Add the chiles and garlic. Sauté for one more minute.

Pour the soaking liquid and lentils into a large saucepan.

Add the bacon and the onion mixture to the saucepan. Bring to a boil, then reduce the heat and simmer for 2 hours, stirring occasionally.

Stir in the ham, carrots, celery, peppercorns, bay leaf, nutmeg, and rosemary. Bring to a boil, then reduce the heat and simmer for 45 to 55 more minutes, stirring occasionally and adding water if necessary.

Remove the bay leaf before serving. Season with salt and pepper to taste. Garnish with cilantro.

Creamy Chicken Soup

A few simple ingredients make a creamy, chile-hot soup in just half an hour.

1/2 cup butter
1/2 cup all-purpose flour
2 cups milk
2 cups water
2 cups chopped, cooked chicken
1/2 cup Hatch green chiles, roasted, peeled,
　　stemmed, seeded, and chopped
1/4 tsp. garlic powder
Salt and freshly ground black pepper

Melt the butter in a large saucepan over medium heat. Add the flour and stir constantly to make a roux until it is the consistency of sand and has a slightly nutty aroma. This will thicken the soup.

Add the milk and water. Whisk to incorporate into the roux.

Add the chicken, chiles, and garlic powder. Bring to a boil, then reduce the heat, cover, and simmer for 30 minutes, stirring occasionally. Season with salt and pepper to taste.

Hatch Beef Stock

Flavored with green chiles and red wine, this beef stock will flavor the Lentil-Ham Soup *and can also be used in any recipe where a beef stock is called for.*

3 pounds beef soup bones, rinsed
4 quarts water
2 celery stalks, sliced
1 carrot, sliced
1 onion, quartered
4 Hatch green chiles, roasted, peeled,
    stemmed, seeded, and chopped
1 garlic clove, crushed
1 bay leaf
1 tsp. dried thyme
1/2 bunch cilantro, rinsed
1/2 tsp. black peppercorns
2 cups red wine

Preheat the oven to 400 degrees. Place the soup bones on a baking sheet and roast them for 90 minutes to 2 hours or until they turn golden brown.

Add the bones and water to a stockpot. Bring to a boil, then reduce the heat to medium and skim the foam that rises to the surface for the first 20 minutes.

Stir in all the remaining ingredients. Cover and simmer for 8 to 12 hours, stirring occasionally. Let the stock cool, then discard the bay leaf and any fat which has accumulated on the top. Strain the stock and use right away for a recipe or freeze for future use.

 This stock freezes well. If you don't have all day to simmer the stock, place it in a crock pot after the boil and skim step.

Green Chile Beef Stew

A classic green chile stew, with a touch of garlic and cumin.

1 pound beef stew cubes
1 medium onion, chopped
3 Hatch green chiles, roasted, peeled,
  stemmed, seeded, and chopped
2 garlic cloves, minced
2 cups chopped tomatoes
5 carrots, coarsely chopped
5 small potatoes, peeled and coarsely chopped
1/4 tsp. ground cumin
1 tsp. salt
1/4 tsp. black pepper
2 T. all-purpose flour
Flour tortillas, warmed

Heat a large saucepan over medium-high heat. Rinse the meat under cold running water and add it to the pan. Brown the meat in its own juices, adding more water if necessary.

Stir in the onion, chiles, garlic, tomatoes, carrots, potatoes, cumin, salt, and pepper.

Sprinkle the flour over. Stir to coat all the ingredients. Add hot water to cover. Bring to a boil, stirring, then reduce the heat, cover, and simmer for an hour or until the meat is tender, stirring occasionally. Serve with warm flour tortillas.

The village of Hatch, New Mexico, is less than 4 square miles of fertile land along the Rio Grande, about 70 miles northwest of El Paso. It sits in the middle of the Hatch valley, which runs along the river from Caballo Lake to Radium Springs.

Green Chile Steak Stew

Tomatillos, bacon, and beer flavor this variation of a green chile stew.

4 slices bacon, coarsely chopped
2 pounds round steak, cut into cubes
3 cups water
3 cups beer
1 cup chopped white onion
2 tomatillos, husked, rinsed, cored, and quartered
1/2 cup chopped cilantro
2 cups Hatch green chiles, roasted, peeled,
   stemmed, seeded, and chopped
1/2 cup tomato sauce
3 garlic cloves, minced
1-1/2 tsp. salt
1 tsp. black pepper
4 new potatoes, scrubbed and cut into cubes
4 large carrots, sliced
Sour cream
Flour tortillas, warmed

Cook the bacon in a large saucepan over medium-high heat until crisp. Remove and drain on paper towels. Set aside. Turn the heat up to high. Add the meat and brown it on all sides.

Add the water and beer. Bring to a boil, then reduce the heat to medium-low and stir in the bacon, onion, tomatillos, cilantro, chiles, tomato sauce, garlic, salt, and pepper. Cook for 45 minutes, stirring occasionally.

Add the potatoes and carrots. Bring to a boil, then reduce the heat and simmer for 20 more minutes or until the vegetables are tender. Ladle into individual soup bowls. Top with a dollop of sour cream. Serve with warm flour tortillas.

Green Chile Pork Stew

The mother of all Hatch green chile recipes. Add more or less chiles to suit your taste.

1 pound pork tenderloin,
 cut into 1-1/2 inch cubes
1 medium onion, chopped
3 celery stalks, chopped
2 medium carrots, chopped
2 medium red potatoes, scrubbed
 and cut into cubes
8 Hatch green chiles, roasted, peeled,
 stemmed, seeded, and chopped
2 tsp. chopped garlic
1 cup chicken broth
1 cup water, or enough to cover
2 T. cornstarch
1/4 cup water
Salt and freshly ground black pepper
1/4 cup chopped cilantro
Cornbread and butter

Place the pork, onion, celery, carrots, potatoes, chiles, garlic, broth, and one cup water, or more to cover, in a large saucepan. Bring to a boil, then reduce the heat, cover, and simmer for 45 minutes, stirring occasionally.

Mix the cornstarch with 1/4 cup water in a small bowl until it forms a smooth paste.

Add the cornstarch mixture. Increase the heat to medium-high and stir until the stew has thickened. Season with salt and pepper to taste.

Ladle into individual soup bowls. Garnish with cilantro.

Serve with warm buttered cornbread.

Slow Picante Soup

Toss all the ingredients into a crock pot and dinner is ready when you come home. Serve with cornbread.

    2 pounds stew beef cubes
    1 (14.5 oz.) can Mexican style tomatoes
    1 (14.5 oz.) can beef broth
    1 (8 oz.) jar picante sauce
    1 (10 oz.) bag frozen corn, thawed
    4 Hatch green chiles, roasted, peeled,
        stemmed, seeded, and chopped
    1 garlic clove, minced
    1/2 tsp. ground cumin
    1/2 tsp. salt
    1/2 tsp. black pepper
    Cornbread and butter

Heat a 12-inch skillet over medium-high heat. Rinse the meat under cold running water and add it to the skillet. Brown the meat in its own juices, adding more water if necessary.

Place the beef, along with any accumulated juices, the tomatoes, broth, picante sauce, corn, chiles, garlic, cumin, salt, and pepper in a crock pot. Stir to mix.

Cook on high for 3 to 4 hours or on low for 6 to 8 hours.

Serve with warm buttered cornbread.

The intense sunlight and cool nights in Hatch, New Mexico, results in the unique and utterly distinct and delicious taste of Hatch chiles.

Veggies, Rice, Beans, Potatoes, and Pasta

Black-Eyed Peas

Black-eyed peas are small beans that have a black spot in the center. This recipe works well with any kind of beans.

3 T. butter
1 small red onion, chopped
1/4 cup chopped red bell pepper
1 T. minced garlic
2 (15 oz.) cans black-eyed peas,
   drained and rinsed
2 Hatch green chiles, roasted, peeled,
   stemmed, seeded, and chopped
1/2 cup mild salsa

Melt the butter in a medium-size saucepan over medium-high heat. Add the onion and bell pepper. Sauté until tender. Add the garlic and sauté for one more minute.

Stir in the black-eyed peas, chiles, and salsa. Bring to a boil, then reduce the heat to low and simmer for 5 minutes.

*To make **Bacon Black-Eyed Peas**, cook 6 slices chopped bacon. Remove and set aside to drain on paper towels. Remove all but 2 T. of the drippings. Omit the butter and continue with the recipe, sautéing the onion, bell pepper, and garlic in the bacon drippings. Crumble the bacon and return it to the pan with the black-eyed peas, chiles, and salsa.*

Chile Mushrooms

If you love mushrooms sautéed in butter with garlic, you'll love this recipe. This is a wonderful side dish served alongside grilled steaks.

1/4 cup butter
1 medium onion, finely chopped
2 garlic cloves, crushed
2 Hatch green chiles, roasted, peeled,
   stemmed, seeded, and chopped
3 (16 oz.) containers button mushrooms
Salt and freshly ground black pepper
1 small bunch cilantro, coarsely chopped

Melt the butter in a 12-inch skillet over medium-high heat. Add the onion, garlic, chiles, and mushrooms. Stir until they are evenly coated with the butter.

Cook, stirring once or twice, until the onion and mushrooms are browned and tender, and the liquid has evaporated. Season with salt and pepper to taste.

Place the mushrooms in a serving bowl. Sprinkle with the cilantro.

 *Most vegetables lose texture and taste if you freeze them, but not Hatch chiles. They actually increase their heat level when frozen. The longer they're in the freezer, the hotter they'll be.*

Cauliflower-Chile Casserole

Cheese and a tomato-chile sauce cover this yummy cauliflower casserole.

> 1 large cauliflower, cut into florets
> 1 large tomato, cored and chopped
> 2 garlic cloves, coarsely chopped
> 3 Hatch green chiles, roasted, peeled,
>   stemmed, seeded, and chopped
> 2 cups shredded Colby Jack cheese
> Salt and freshly ground black pepper

Preheat the oven to 350 degrees. Lightly spray a 13 x 9 glass baking dish with nonstick cooking spray. Set aside.

Cook the cauliflower in a large saucepan of boiling water until tender. Drain.

While this is cooking, place the tomato, garlic, and chiles in a blender. Process until smooth.

Place the cauliflower florets in the prepared baking dish. Spoon the sauce over and top with the cheese. Bake for 10 minutes or until the cheese is melted.

Season with salt and pepper to taste.

Chile Rellenos with Sauce

There are many variations of Chile Rellenos. They can be stuffed with cheese, vegetables, meat, or any combination of these. They are most often served with a tomato-based sauce. They can be a little tricky to stuff, as they tend to fall apart, but are well worth the effort.

6 whole Hatch green chiles
3 T. butter
1 large onion, thinly sliced
1-1/2 cups coarsely chopped tomatoes
1/2 cup chicken broth
Salt and freshly ground black pepper
1-3/4 cups shredded Cheddar cheese
1 large egg, separated
1/4 cup all-purpose flour
1/4 cup vegetable oil
1 (8 oz.) container sour cream

Make a slit down one side of each chile. Do not cut all the way through. Remove the seeds through the slits, keeping the chiles whole. Dry them gently with paper towels and set aside.

Melt the butter in a 12-inch skillet over medium heat. Add the onion and sauté until tender. Add the tomatoes and broth. Cook for 5 more minutes. Season with salt and pepper to taste. Set the sauce aside and keep warm.

Mold the cheese into six sausage-shaped logs. Place them into the chiles. Fold the chiles tightly around the cheese filling and flatten slightly. Set aside.

Beat the egg white in a medium-size bowl until it peaks. Add the yolk and beat just to incorporate.

Put the flour on a dinner plate and roll the chiles in the flour to dust them all over.

Holding the stem, twist each chile in the egg mixture to coat it thickly.

Heat the oil in a deep frying pan over high heat. Cook the chiles, two or three at a time, for 2 minutes on each side, using tongs or a spatula to turn.

Spoon the sauce on individual dinner plates. Place a chile on top of the sauce and top with a dollop of sour cream.

Spicy Spinach

Spinach, bacon, onion, and garlic are a classic combination. Add some Hatch and you take it over the top. This can be served as a side dish or as a wilted spinach salad.

3 slices bacon, cut into small pieces
1/4 cup minced onion
3 Hatch green chiles, roasted, peeled,
   stemmed, seeded, and chopped
1 garlic clove, minced
1/4 tsp. chili powder
1 (10 oz.) package fresh baby spinach
Salt and freshly ground black pepper

Cook the bacon in a 12-inch skillet over medium-high heat until almost crisp.

Add the onion, chiles, and garlic. Sauté until the bacon is crisp and the onion is tender. Season with the chili powder.

Reduce the heat to medium. Add the spinach in batches and cover the pan to let the spinach wilt, stirring after each addition.

Season with salt and pepper to taste.

Bacon Green Beans

Top these with Cheddar cheese for extra flavor.

3 cups fresh green beans
3 slices bacon
2 Hatch green chiles, roasted, peeled,
    stemmed, seeded, and chopped
1 large tomato, cored and chopped
1/2 cup water
Salt and freshly ground black pepper

Remove the strings from the green beans. Cut off the ends, then slice into matchsticks. Set aside.

Cook the bacon in a 12-inch skillet over medium-high heat until crisp. Remove and drain on paper towels. Let cool slightly, then crumble the bacon into a small bowl and set aside.

Add the chiles to the skillet and sauté for one minute in the bacon drippings. Drain.

Add the tomato and water. Bring to a boil, then reduce the heat and simmer for one minute.

Add the green beans and cook for 10 minutes or until tender, stirring occasionally and adding more water if necessary.

Drain the green bean mixture and place it in a serving bowl. Season with salt and pepper to taste. Sprinkle the crumbled bacon over and toss lightly.

Hatch chiles are a fruit, but are classified as a vegetable in New Mexico. Chiles are a member of the nightshade family.

Chiliquile Calabacitas

Zucchini, black beans, tomatoes, corn, Hatch chiles, tortillas, and cheese combine to make a totally delicious casserole.

1 T. olive oil
1 medium onion, diced
1 medium zucchini, shredded
1 (15 oz.) can black beans,
    drained and rinsed
1 (14.5 oz.) can diced tomatoes
1-1/2 cups frozen corn, thawed
2 Hatch green chiles, roasted, peeled,
    stemmed, seeded, and chopped
1 tsp. ground cumin
1/2 tsp. salt
12 (6-inch) corn tortillas, quartered
1 (14 oz.) can red or green enchilada sauce
1-1/4 cups shredded Cheddar cheese

Preheat the oven to 400 degrees. Lightly spray a 13 x 9 glass baking dish with nonstick cooking spray. Set aside.

Heat the oil in a 12-inch skillet over medium-high heat. Add the onion and sauté until tender.

Stir in the zucchini, beans, tomatoes, corn, chiles, cumin, and salt. Cook until the vegetables are heated through, stirring occasionally.

Place half the tortilla pieces in the prepared baking dish. Spoon half the vegetable mixture over, half the enchilada sauce, and half the cheese. Repeat. Cover with aluminum foil and bake for 15 minutes.

Remove from the oven and uncover. Return to the oven and bake for 10 more minutes or until the cheese is melted.

Queso Calabacitas

This flavorful veggie dish is a combination of onion, corn, chiles, and zucchini baked together in a cheesy goodness.

2 T. butter
1 large onion, chopped
1 (15 oz.) can corn, drained
4 Hatch green chiles, roasted, peeled,
    stemmed, seeded, and chopped
2 medium zucchini, sliced
2 cups shredded Cheddar cheese, divided

Preheat the oven to 350 degrees. Lightly spray a 3-quart glass casserole dish with nonstick cooking spray. Set aside.

Melt the butter in a 12-inch skillet over medium heat. Add the onion and sauté until tender. Remove to a medium-size bowl.

Stir in the corn, chiles, zucchini, and 1-1/2 cups of the cheese. Spoon the mixture into the prepared baking dish.

Top with the remaining cheese and bake for 30 minutes.

Simply Squash

A delicious veggie side dish, spicy from chiles and covered with Cheddar cheese.

>   3 T. olive oil
>   1 medium onion, chopped
>   6 yellow squash, sliced into
>   one-half inch rings
>   1/2 tsp. salt
>   2 garlic cloves, minced
>   3 Hatch green chiles, roasted, peeled,
>   stemmed, seeded, and chopped
>   1-1/2 cups shredded Cheddar cheese

Preheat the oven to 350 degrees. Lightly spray a 13 x 9 glass baking dish with nonstick cooking spray. Set aside.

Heat the oil in a 12-inch skillet over medium heat. Add the onion and squash. Season with salt. Sauté until tender.

Add the garlic and chiles. Sauté for one more minute.

Place the mixture in the prepared baking dish. Cover with aluminum foil and bake for 30 minutes.

Remove from the oven and uncover. Sprinkle the cheese over the top. Return to the oven and bake for 10 more minutes or until the cheese is melted and lightly brown.

Hatch chiles are young chiles; they haven't been around that long. They were born around 1912, when New Mexicans began cultivating them. The ancient Anasazi Indians have used chiles in New Mexico from the year 400.

Baked Zucchini Boats

These are so good that you might want to make a meal out of them instead of a veggie side dish.

> 3 zucchini, scrubbed and sliced
>   in half lengthwise
> 6 T. butter, divided
> 1 small onion, chopped
> 1 garlic clove, chopped
> 2 large tomatoes, chopped
> 2 Hatch green chiles, roasted, peeled,
>   stemmed, seeded, and chopped
> 3/4 cup bread crumbs
> 1/4 cup Parmesan cheese
> Salt and freshly ground black pepper
> 1 T. chopped cilantro

Preheat the oven to 350 degrees. Lightly spray a 13 x 9 glass baking dish with nonstick cooking spray. Set aside.

Scoop out the zucchini pulp, leaving the shells intact. Set the shells and pulp aside.

Melt 3 T. of the butter in a 12-inch skillet over medium heat. Add the onion and sauté until tender. Add the garlic and sauté for one more minute.

Stir in the zucchini pulp, tomatoes, and chiles. Cook for two more minutes.

Fill the zucchini shells with this mixture. Place them in the prepared baking dish and set aside.

Melt the remaining butter in the skillet. Stir in the bread crumbs, cheese, the salt and pepper to taste, and the cilantro.

Top the zucchini with the bread crumb mixture. Cover with aluminum foil and bake for 30 minutes.

Chile Corn Casserole

Green chiles and corn are a natural together.

Butter, for the baking dish
1 cup sour cream
1 tsp. chicken bouillon granules
1/2 tsp. seasoned salt
1/4 tsp. dry mustard
2 Hatch green chiles, roasted, peeled,
    stemmed, seeded, and chopped
2 T. butter, melted
1 (32 oz.) package frozen corn, thawed
1/2 cup crushed tortilla chips

Preheat the oven to 350 degrees. Lightly butter a 13 x 9 glass baking dish. Set aside.

Combine the sour cream, bouillon, seasoned salt, dry mustard, chiles, melted butter, and corn in a medium-size bowl.

Place the mixture in the prepared baking dish. Sprinkle the crushed tortilla chips over the top.

Bake for 30 minutes or until heated through.

Chile Corn

Green onion, tomatoes, and Monterey Jack cheese add dimension and flavor to this delicious veggie side dish.

2 T. butter
1/2 cup chopped green onion
2 Hatch green chiles, roasted, peeled,
   stemmed, seeded, and chopped
1 (14.5 oz.) can diced tomatoes
2-1/2 cups frozen corn, thawed
1-1/2 cups shredded Monterey Jack cheese

Melt the butter in a 12-inch skillet over medium heat. Add the onion and sauté until tender.

Add the chiles and tomatoes. Cook for 5 minutes to reduce the sauce.

Add the corn and cook for 10 more minutes or until the corn is tender. Remove the skillet from the heat and stir in the cheese until melted.

Classic Chile Corn

A favorite recipe featuring onion and red bell pepper.

3 T. butter, divided
1 cup chopped onion
2-1/2 cups frozen corn, thawed
2 Hatch green chiles, roasted, peeled,
   stemmed, seeded, and chopped
1/2 cup chopped red bell pepper
Salt and freshly ground black pepper

Melt 1 T. of the butter in a 12-inch skillet over medium heat. Add the onion and sauté until tender.

Melt the remaining butter in the skillet. Add the corn, chiles, and bell pepper. Cook for 10 minutes or until the vegetables are tender and the onion is lightly browned. Season with salt and pepper to taste.

 To make **Classic Chile Corn and Black Beans,** *add one (15 oz.) can black beans, drained and rinsed.*

Cayenne Chile Corn

The cayenne adds an extra kick of heat and is perfect for flavor and color.

2 T. vegetable oil
1 medium onion, chopped
3 cups frozen corn, thawed
4 Hatch green chiles, roasted, peeled,
   stemmed, seeded, and chopped
6 garlic cloves, minced
1 T. chili powder
1 tsp. cayenne pepper
Salt and freshly ground black pepper
2 T. fresh lime juice

Heat the oil in a 12-inch skillet over medium-high heat. Add the onion and sauté until tender.

Add the corn. Cook for 10 minutes, stirring occasionally. Add the chiles and garlic. Sauté for one more minute.

Season with the chili powder, cayenne pepper, and the salt and pepper to taste. Squirt in the lime juice just before serving.

Over Labor Day weekend, Hatch, New Mexico, hosts the annual Hatch Chile Festival which features a parade, a chile eating contest and tons of freshly roasted Hatch chiles for sale. Approximately 3,000 people from all over the world attend every year.

Hatch Hominy

Red bell peppers and green Hatch chiles make this a colorful side dish.

1 T. vegetable oil
1 small onion, chopped
1 red bell pepper, chopped
1 garlic clove, minced
5 Hatch green chiles, roasted, peeled, stemmed, seeded, and chopped
1 (14.5 oz.) can diced tomatoes
1 (15.5 oz.) can hominy, drained
1/2 tsp. chili powder
1/2 tsp. cayenne pepper

Heat the oil in a 12-inch skillet over medium-high heat. Add the onion and bell pepper. Sauté until tender.

Add the garlic and chiles. Sauté for one more minute.

Stir in the tomatoes, hominy, chili powder and cayenne pepper. Bring to a boil, then reduce the heat and simmer for 10 minutes, stirring occasionally.

Hatch, New Mexico, was named after General Edward Hatch, who served under Ulysses S. Grant.

Eggplant Casserole

Hatch chiles, cumin, and cayenne pepper give this Southwest version of Eggplant Parmesan a nice kick.

1 large eggplant
Salt, as needed
1/3 cup vegetable oil
1 (19 oz.) can enchilada sauce
4 Hatch green chiles, roasted, peeled,
   stemmed, seeded, and chopped
1/2 cup thinly sliced green onion
1/2 tsp. ground cumin
1/2 tsp. cayenne pepper
1/2 tsp. garlic salt
1-1/2 cups shredded Monterey Jack cheese
1 (8 oz.) container sour cream

Cut the unpeeled eggplant into 1/2-inch slices, crosswise. Sprinkle them lightly with salt and place them in a colander to drain for 20 minutes.

Preheat the oven to 450 degrees. Lightly spray a 13 x 9 glass baking dish with nonstick cooking spray. Set aside.

Place the drained eggplant slices on a large baking sheet. Brush both sides with the vegetable oil. Bake for 15 minutes or until they are lightly browned and crisp. Remove from the oven and reduce the temperature to 350 degrees.

While this is cooking, combine the enchilada sauce, chiles, onion, cumin, cayenne pepper, and garlic salt in a medium-size saucepan. Simmer for 10 minutes.

Line the prepared baking dish with half the eggplant slices. Spoon half the enchilada sauce mixture over. Sprinkle with half the cheese. Repeat. Bake for 25 minutes or the cheese is lightly brown. Serve with sour cream on the side.

Chunky Eggplant

Simmered on the stove, this is a delicious side dish that can be served with any meal.

    1 eggplant, cut into chunks
    3 T. fajita seasoning
    3 T. vegetable oil
    4 Hatch green chiles, roasted, peeled,
        stemmed, seeded, and coarsely chopped
    1 medium onion, coarsely chopped
    2 large ripe tomatoes, coarsely chopped
    2 tsp. paprika

Place the eggplant chunks in a medium-size bowl. Sprinkle with the fajita seasoning and stir to coat. Place them in a colander to drain for 10 minutes.

Heat the oil in a 12-inch skillet over medium-high heat. Add the eggplant, chiles, and onion. Sauté until the vegetables are tender.

Stir in the tomatoes and paprika. Bring to a boil, then reduce the heat and simmer for 20 minutes, stirring occasionally.

Green Rice

This rice is green from the chiles and cilantro.

2 Hatch green chiles, roasted, peeled,
   stemmed, seeded, and chopped
1 green bell pepper, roasted, peeled,
   stemmed, seeded, and chopped
1 garlic clove, coarsely chopped
1 bunch cilantro, coarsely chopped
2 cups chicken broth
2 T. vegetable oil
1 small onion, finely chopped
1 cup long-grain white rice
Salt and freshly ground black pepper

Put the chiles, bell pepper, garlic, cilantro, and broth into a blender. Blend until smooth.

Heat the oil in a 12-inch skillet over medium heat. Add the onion and rice. Cook, stirring occasionally, for 5 minutes or until the rice is golden and the onion is tender.

Stir in the chile-broth mixture. Bring to a boil, then reduce the heat, cover, and simmer for 20 to 25 minutes or until all the liquid is absorbed and the rice is tender. Season with salt and pepper to taste.

Chile-Cheese Rice

This baked rice casserole is topped with melted cheesy goodness.

    2 T. butter
    1 cup long grain white rice
    1/2 small onion, finely minced
    2 Hatch green chiles, roasted, peeled,
        stemmed, seeded, and chopped
    1 garlic clove, minced
    1/4 tsp. salt
    1/4 tsp. ground cumin
    1 (14 oz.) can chicken broth
    1 cup shredded Colby Jack cheese, divided
    4 T. chopped cilantro

Preheat the oven to 375 degrees. Lightly spray a 13 x 9 glass baking dish with nonstick cooking spray. Set aside.

Melt the butter in a 12-inch skillet over medium heat. Add the rice. Cook, stirring, until the rice begins to brown.

Add the onion and sauté for one minute with the rice. Stir in the chiles, garlic, salt, and cumin.

Add the broth. Bring to a boil, then reduce the heat, cover, and simmer for 15 minutes or until the rice is almost tender.

Remove the pan from the heat. Stir in 3/4 cup of the cheese and the cilantro. Place in the prepared baking dish. Top with the remaining cheese. Bake for 10 to 15 minutes or until the rice is tender and the cheese is melted.

This rice also makes a great cold rice salad by itself or wrap in a Romaine lettuce leaf for a salad wrap. You can also use it in a stuffed bell pepper recipe.

Rice and Beans

Rice and beans are a perfect accompaniment to every meal.

1 cup tomato juice
1/2 tsp. garlic powder
1/4 tsp. cayenne pepper
1/4 tsp. ground cumin
2 Hatch green chiles, roasted, peeled,
   stemmed, seeded, and chopped
1 (15.5 oz.) can dark red kidney beans,
   drained, rinsed, and slightly mashed
3 cups cooked white rice, hot
Salt and freshly ground black pepper
1 cup shredded Cheddar cheese

Heat the tomato juice, garlic powder, cayenne pepper, cumin, chiles, and beans to boiling in a medium-size saucepan. Stir to mix.

Reduce the heat to low. Cover and cook for 5 minutes to blend the flavors, stirring occasionally.

Stir in the cooked rice and heat through. Season with salt and pepper to taste. Sprinkle with the cheese.

 Optional Additions: Sauté 1/2 cup each onion and green bell pepper in 2 T. butter then follow the recipe. For extra heat add a serrano or jalapeño pepper.

Black Bean Lasagna

This lasagna, southwest style, offers a vegetarian take on the classic version.

1 (15 oz.) container ricotta cheese
1/3 cup shredded Cheddar cheese
1 medium egg
1/4 cup milk
4 T. chopped cilantro, divided
1 (28 oz.) can enchilada sauce
9 (8-inch) flour tortillas
2 (15 oz.) cans black beans, drained and rinsed
4 Hatch green chiles, roasted, peeled,
    stemmed, seeded, and chopped
1-1/2 cups fresh chopped spinach
2 cups shredded Monterey Jack cheese

Preheat the oven to 350 degrees.

Combine the ricotta and Cheddar cheeses with the egg, milk, and half the cilantro in a medium-size bowl.

Spread a thin layer of the enchilada sauce in a 13 x 9 glass baking dish. Place three tortillas, overlapping them if needed, on the bottom of the baking dish. Cover with 1/3 each of the beans, chiles, spinach, ricotta-Cheddar mixture, and the Monterey Jack cheese. Cover with 1/3 of the enchilada sauce. Repeat twice to make three layers. Sprinkle the top with the remaining cilantro. Cover with aluminum foil and bake for 30 minutes.

Remove from the oven and uncover. Return to the oven and bake for 10 more minutes or until the cheese is melted.

Add one pound of cooked lean ground beef to make a meaty meal.

Beer Beans

The beans practically cook themselves with just a little help from you. Soak the beans the night before.

1-1/4 cups dry pinto beans
1 pound smoked ham hock
1 medium onion, finely diced, divided
1 T. vegetable oil
4 Hatch green chiles, roasted, peeled,
    stemmed, seeded, and chopped
1 T. cumin seed
1 T. chili powder
1 (12 oz.) can beer
1 (14.5 oz.) can diced tomatoes
2 T. chopped cilantro
Salt, to taste

Rinse the beans and soak them in a large bowl of cold water overnight. Drain in a colander, rinse under cold running water, and drain again.

Simmer the ham hock in 6 cups water in a large saucepan for 1-1/2 hours. Skim the fat or refrigerate until the fat can be scraped off. Reserve the broth.

Place the ham hock, broth, half the onion, and the beans in a 6-quart stockpot. Bring to a boil, then reduce the heat and simmer for 2 hours or until the beans are tender, stirring occasionally. Add more boiling water if the mixture becomes dry. Remove the ham hock. Chop any remaining meat and return it to the pan.

Heat the oil in a 12-inch skillet over medium-high heat. Add the remaining onion, chiles, cumin, and chili powder. Sauté until the onion is tender. Add the beer, tomatoes, and cilantro. Cook for 5 more minutes. Add the beer mixture to the bean mixture. Season with salt to taste.

Charro Beans

Charro beans are whole beans, not mashed.

2 (15.5 oz.) cans pinto beans, drained and rinsed
1/2 cup chicken broth
6 Hatch green chiles, roasted, peeled,
    stemmed, seeded, and chopped
2 medium tomatoes, peeled and chopped
1 tsp. ground cinnamon
3 slices bacon, coarsely chopped
1 medium onion, chopped
2 garlic cloves, crushed

Place the beans and broth in a large saucepan. Bring to a boil and cook for 5 minutes, stirring occasionally.

Reduce the heat to medium. Stir in the chiles, tomatoes, and cinnamon. Cook for 10 more minutes, stirring occasionally.

While this is cooking, cook the bacon in a 12-inch skillet over medium-high heat until crisp. Remove and drain on paper towels. Add the onion and sauté until the onion is tender. Add the garlic and sauté for one more minute. Drain.

Add the onion-garlic mixture and the bacon to the beans. Stir to mix.

Just as it's said that beans are good for the heart (you know how the jingle goes), so it goes that Hatch chiles are good for your health. Chiles are used in the making of teas and lozenges for the treatment of a sore throat, and capsaicinoids, the chemical that makes chile peppers hot, are used in muscle patches for sore and aching muscles.

Drunken Beans

The beans are cooked in beer. They are also referred to as frijoles borracho which means drunken beans. The beans are whole and are served in their broth.

2 cups dried pinto beans
1/2 pound bacon, chopped
1 large white onion, chopped
1 T. dried oregano
1 garlic clove, finely chopped
1-1/2 quarts water
6 Hatch green chiles, roasted, peeled,
    stemmed, seeded, and chopped
1 (12 oz.) bottle dark beer, such as Dos Equis
2 tsp. salt, or more to taste

Rinse the beans and soak them in a large bowl of cold water overnight. Drain in a colander, rinse under cold running water, and drain again. Set aside.

Preheat the oven to 300 degrees.

Cook the bacon, onion, oregano, and garlic in a Dutch oven over medium-high heat, stirring, until the bacon is crisp and the onion is lightly browned. Drain. Add the beans, water, chiles, and beer. Bring to a boil and let boil for one minute.

Place the pan in the middle of the oven and bake for 1-1/2 to 2 hours or until the beans are tender. Add additional water if the beans begin to dry out. The mixture will be soupy.

Remove from the oven and add the salt to taste. Stir to mix.

Season beans with salt to taste when they're done cooking. Adding salt during cooking toughens the beans.

Quickie Pintos

This quick and easy recipe starts with a can of pinto beans.
The additional ingredients add flavor and spicy heat.

>2 tsp. olive oil
>1 small onion, chopped
>1 garlic clove, minced
>2 Hatch green chiles, roasted, peeled,
>   stemmed, seeded, and chopped
>1/2 tsp. chili powder
>1 (15.5 oz.) can pinto beans,
>   drained and rinsed
>1/2 cup water
>1/4 tsp. ground cumin
>1/4 tsp. salt
>1 T. chopped cilantro

Heat the oil in a medium-size saucepan over medium-high heat. Add the onion, garlic, chiles, and chili powder. Sauté until the vegetables are tender.

Stir in the beans, water, cumin, and salt. Coarsely mash half of the beans in the pan. Reduce the heat and simmer until heated through. Stir in the cilantro.

Perfect Pintos

Pintos are the bean of choice for many people.

1-1/2 cups dried pinto beans
2 medium onions, coarsely chopped
10 garlic cloves, coarsely chopped
10 slices bacon, coarsely chopped
6 Hatch green chiles, roasted, peeled,
    stemmed, seeded, and chopped
1 small bunch cilantro, divided
Salt and freshly ground black pepper

Rinse the beans and soak them in a large bowl of cold water overnight. Drain in a colander, rinse under cold running water, and drain again.

Put 2-1/2 cups of water in a large stockpot. Bring to a boil, then add the beans. Bring to a boil again. Add the onions, garlic, bacon, and chiles. Bring to a boil again, stir to mix, then reduce the heat and simmer for 1-1/2 hours or until the beans are tender and there is only a little liquid remaining, stirring occasionally.

Place one cup of the beans and a 1/4 cup of the liquid into a blender. Process until smooth. Return the blended beans to the stockpot. Stir in most of the cilantro. Season with salt and pepper to taste.

Ladle the beans into individual serving bowls. Sprinkle with the remaining cilantro.

Peasant Potatoes

These potatoes add a spicy heat to your meal. Leftovers are great for breakfast, served with eggs and chorizo, or as a side dish for Huevos Rancheros.

> 4 T. vegetable oil, divided
> 1 medium onion, finely chopped
> 1 pound yellow potatoes, scrubbed
>   and cut into one-half inch cubes
> 6 Hatch green chiles, roasted, peeled,
>   stemmed, seeded, and chopped
> 1 cup shredded Cheddar cheese
> 2 T. chopped cilantro

Heat half the oil in a 12-inch skillet over medium heat. Add the onion and sauté until tender.

Add the potatoes. Stir to coat them with the oil, then cover the pan and cook for 20 minutes or until the potatoes are tender and lightly browned, turning them with a spatula occasionally to prevent them from sticking to the bottom.

Push the potatoes to the side of the skillet, turn the heat up to high and add the remaining oil.

When the oil is hot, spread out the potatoes. Cook for 5 to 10 minutes, stirring carefully so the potatoes turn golden brown all over but do not break up.

Sprinkle with the chiles, cheese, and cilantro. Cover the skillet until the cheese is melted.

One fresh, medium-sized green chile has as much Vitamin C as six oranges.

Pimiento Potatoes

Pimientos are a small, sweet red pepper, similar to, but more flavorful than a bell pepper. This dish is reminiscent of scalloped potatoes.

Butter, for the baking dish
1/3 cup butter
3 T. all-purpose flour
2 cups milk
2 cups shredded Monterey
   Jack cheese, divided
1 (2 oz.) jar diced pimientos, drained
2 Hatch green chiles, roasted, peeled,
   stemmed, seeded, and chopped
1/2 tsp. salt
3 cups peeled, thinly sliced potatoes

Preheat the oven to 350 degrees. Lightly butter a 13 x 9 glass baking dish. Set aside.

Melt 1/3 cup butter in a medium saucepan over low heat. Add the flour, stirring until smooth, then add the milk. Cook, stirring constantly, until the mixture is slightly thickened.

Stir in 1-1/2 cups of the cheese. Remove the pan from the heat and stir until the cheese melts. Stir in the pimientos, chiles, and salt.

Place half the potato slices in the prepared baking dish. Top with half the cheese mixture. Repeat. Cover with aluminum foil and bake for 20 minutes. Remove from the oven and uncover. Return to the oven and bake for 40 more minutes.

Remove from the oven, sprinkle with the remaining cheese and return to the oven. Bake for 10 more minutes or until the cheese is melted and lightly brown.

Chile Cheese Potatoes

These potatoes are baked in a flavorful chile-cheese sauce.

3 pounds red potatoes, scrubbed
1 T. olive oil
5 Hatch green chiles, roasted, peeled,
    stemmed, seeded, and chopped
1 medium onion, chopped
2 cups whipping cream
1 cup milk
2 garlic cloves
Salt and freshly ground black pepper
2-1/2 cups shredded sharp Cheddar cheese

Cook the potatoes in a large saucepan of lightly-salted boiling water for 10 minutes or until barely tender. Drain the potatoes in a colander and let cool completely.

When cool enough to handle, peel and slice the potatoes into one-half inch rounds. Place in a large bowl and set aside.

Heat the oil in a 12-inch skillet over medium-high heat. Add the chiles and onion. Sauté until the onion is tender. Place the mixture in a food processor or a blender.

Add the cream, milk, and garlic to the chile-onion mixture. Blend to form a thick sauce.

Season the sauce with salt and pepper to taste. Pour the sauce over the potatoes. Stir gently to coat.

Preheat the oven to 350 degrees. Lightly spray a 13 x 9 glass baking dish with nonstick cooking spray.

Overlap half the potatoes in the bottom of the prepared baking dish. Sprinkle with half the cheese. Add the remaining potatoes and any remaining sauce, then top with the remaining cheese. Bake for 30 minutes or until heated through and the cheese is lightly brown.

Green Chile Potatoes

If you have leftover potatoes, they're great for breakfast, smashed into potato patties and fried along with your eggs.

> 2 pounds red potatoes,
>   scrubbed and chopped
> 1 cup sour cream
> 1/2 cup milk
> 6 Hatch green chiles, roasted, peeled,
>   stemmed, seeded, and chopped
> Salt and freshly ground black pepper

Cook the potatoes in a large saucepan of lightly-salted boiling water for 15 minutes or until soft.

Drain, then return the potatoes to the pan. Mash with a potato masher until the potatoes are slightly chunky.

Stir in the sour cream, milk, and chiles. Season with salt and pepper to taste.

Want to lose some weight? Eat more Hatch chiles. This is not a difficult thing to do. Hatch chiles burn calories by triggering a thermodynamic burn in the body, which speeds up the metabolism.

Skillet Potatoes

These are started on the stove and finished in the oven so you'll need a cast iron skillet or an oven-proof skillet.

    4 T. butter, divided
    1 medium onion, diced
    2 garlic cloves, minced
    2 Hatch green chiles, roasted, peeled,
        stemmed, seeded, and chopped
    2 pounds potatoes, peeled and
        cut into one-half inch cubes
    1 tsp. ground cumin
    1/4 tsp. cayenne pepper
    Salt and freshly ground black pepper
    1 cup half-and-half

Preheat the oven to 350 degrees.

Melt 2 T. of the butter in an oven-proof, 14-inch skillet. Add the onion and sauté until the onion is tender. Add the garlic and chiles. Sauté for one more minute.

Stir in the potatoes, cumin, cayenne pepper, and the salt and pepper to taste.

Pour the half-and-half over the potatoes. Cover the skillet with aluminum foil. Place in the oven and bake for one hour.

Remove from the oven and uncover. Dot the remaining butter on top of the potatoes. Place the skillet under the broiler for 2 to 3 minutes or until the potatoes are starting to brown on the top.

 Garnish with cilantro, parsley, or finely minced green onion.

Chile Cheese Fries

Smothered with a chile cheese gravy that includes bacon, tomatoes, and onions, these fries are a meal unto themselves.

> 3 large baking potatoes, peeled,
>   cut in half, then cut into strips
> 1/2 cup vegetable oil
> 5 slices bacon, diced
> 1 large onion, chopped
> 1 cup chopped tomato
> 6 Hatch green chiles, roasted, peeled,
>   stemmed, seeded, and chopped
> 1/4 cup milk
> 3 T. water
> 1 (8 oz.) package Muenster or
>   Monterey Jack cheese, shredded

Cook the potatoes in a large saucepan of lightly-salted boiling water for 5 minutes. Drain and pat dry with paper towels. Set aside.

Heat the oil in a deep skillet over medium-high heat.

While the oil is heating, cook the bacon and onion in a 12-inch skillet over medium-high heat until the bacon is crisp and the onion is tender. Drain. Reduce the heat to medium. Add the tomato and chiles. Cover and cook for 5 minutes.

While this is cooking, fry the potatoes until they are golden brown and crisp. Remove with a slotted spoon. Drain on paper towels, then place on serving plates.

Stir the milk and water into the bacon mixture. Cook for 3 more minutes, stirring.

Add the cheese and stir until it melts. Pour the mixture over the hot potatoes.

Potato Circles

Perfect as a side dish or with a burger.

1/4 cup vegetable oil
6 red potatoes, scrubbed and cut into thin circles
1 medium onion, cut into rings
3 Hatch green chiles, roasted, peeled,
    stemmed, seeded, and chopped
Salt and freshly ground black pepper

Heat the oil in a 12-inch skillet over medium-high heat. Add the potato circles and onion rings. Fry for 15 minutes or until almost crispy, stirring frequently.

Add the chiles and fry until the potatoes are tender and crispy. Season with salt and pepper to taste.

Chile Papas

This potato casserole is awesome!

2 large baking potatoes, peeled and sliced
1 medium onion, coarsely chopped
2 Hatch green chiles, roasted, peeled,
    stemmed, seeded, and chopped
1 (10 oz.) can enchilada sauce
1 cup shredded Monterey Jack cheese

Preheat the oven to 350 degrees. Lightly spray a 13 x 9 glass baking dish with nonstick cooking spray.

Make a layer of potatoes, onion, and chiles in the prepared baking dish. Spoon some of the enchilada sauce over. Top with some of the cheese. Continue to layer, topping the final layer with the remaining cheese. Cover with aluminum foil and bake for 40 minutes or until the potatoes are tender. Remove from the oven, uncover, and bake for 10 more minutes to brown the cheese.

Poncho Baked Potato

This potato is loaded with beef, gravy, beans, and chiles.

4 large baking potatoes, scrubbed
1-1/2 pounds lean ground beef
1 small onion, finely chopped
1 (10.25 oz.) can beef gravy
1 (15.5 oz.) can dark red kidney
   beans, drained and rinsed
2 T. chili powder
2 T. ketchup
1 garlic clove, minced
2 Hatch green chiles, roasted, peeled,
   stemmed, seeded, and chopped
Butter for the baked potatoes
Salt and freshly ground black pepper
1 cup shredded Cheddar cheese
1 cup shredded Monterey Jack cheese
1/4 cup chopped cilantro

Preheat the oven to 350 degrees. Prick each potato several times with the tines of a fork. Place in the oven and cook for one hour, 15 minutes.

During the last 30 minutes of baking time, brown the ground beef with the onion in a 12-inch skillet over medium-high heat.

Add the gravy, beans, chili powder, ketchup, garlic, and chiles. Bring to a boil, then reduce the heat and simmer for 20 minutes, stirring occasionally.

Remove the potatoes from the oven and split them lengthwise. Butter them and sprinkle with salt and pepper to taste. Spoon the beef and gravy mixture over the baked potatoes. Sprinkle with the Cheddar and Monterey Jack cheeses. Garnish with cilantro.

Potato Skins

What's better than bacon, cheese, and Hatch chiles on a baked potato, topped with sour cream?

> 4 large baking potatoes, scrubbed
> 1 T. vegetable oil
> 1 cup cubed Mexican Velveeta cheese
> 1 tsp. Tabasco sauce
> 10 slices bacon, crisp-cooked and crumbled
> 4 green onions, chopped, divided
> 2 Hatch green chiles, roasted, peeled,
>   stemmed, seeded, and chopped
> 1 cup shredded Cheddar cheese
> Sour cream

Preheat the oven to 350 degrees. Prick each potato several times with the tines of a fork. Rub each potato with the oil. Place them in the oven and cook for one hour, 15 minutes. Remove the potatoes and turn the oven to broil.

Split the baked potatoes in half lengthwise. Scoop out the pulp and reserve it for another use. (Or mix the pulp with butter, season with salt and pepper to taste, and return it to the potato skins.)

Place the Velveeta cheese in a small bowl and melt it in the microwave. Stir in the Tabasco sauce.

Place equal amounts of the cheese mixture in each potato skin. Top with equal amounts of bacon, 3/4 of the onions, and the chiles. Top with the Cheddar cheese. Broil the potato skins until the cheese is bubbling.

Sprinkle the remaining onions over. Top with a dollop of sour cream.

Mac 'n' Cheese

This recipe brings the lowly macaroni and cheese up to an entirely new, and delicious, level. You'll need a deep, 12-inch chef's skillet for this recipe.

1 tsp. olive oil
1/2 cup minced onion
1 garlic clove, minced
3 cups milk
1-1/2 sticks butter
1/2 cup all-purpose flour
1 tsp. salt
2 tsp. black pepper
2 tsp. cayenne pepper
2 tsp. ground nutmeg
6 cups shredded Monterey Jack cheese, divided
3 Hatch green chiles, roasted, peeled,
    stemmed, seeded, and chopped
1 (16 oz.) box elbow macaroni, cooked
    al dente and drained
6 slices bacon, crisp-cooked and crumbled
1/2 cup bread crumbs

Preheat the oven to 375 degrees. Lightly spray a 13 x 9 glass baking dish with nonstick cooking spray. Set aside.

Heat the oil in an 8-inch skillet over medium heat. Add the onion and sauté until tender. Add the garlic and sauté for one more minute.

Pour the milk into a medium-size saucepan. Heat over medium heat.

While the milk is heating, melt the butter in a large saucepan over medium-low heat. Add the flour and the onion-garlic mixture. Whisk until well incorporated.

Pour the warmed milk into the butter mixture. Whisk until the mixture thickens. Remove the pan from the heat. Season with salt, pepper, cayenne pepper, and nutmeg. Add 5-1/2 cups of the cheese and the chiles. Mix well.

Place the cooked pasta in the prepared baking dish. Pour the cheese sauce over the top. Stir to mix. Sprinkle with the bacon, bread crumbs, and remaining cheese. Bake for 30 minutes or until the cheese is lightly brown.

Pesto Pasta

Serve this over any type of pasta such as fettuccini or penne.

1 cup Hatch green chiles, roasted, peeled,
   stemmed, seeded, and chopped
1 cup chopped cilantro
1/3 cup pine nuts
1/2 cup grated Parmesan cheese
1/2 cup virgin olive oil
2 cups cooked pasta, hot

Place the chiles, cilantro, pine nuts, and cheese in a blender or a food processor. Slowly drizzle in the olive oil while blending. Serve over hot cooked pasta.

 Use chopped fresh basil or parsley instead of the cilantro.

Potato Spuds

The addition of Hatch chiles make this potato salad special. Serve it warm or cold.

> 6 large potatoes, peeled and diced
> 1 cup mayonnaise
> 1 tsp. dill weed
> 1 cup Hatch green chiles, roasted, peeled, stemmed, seeded, and chopped
> 1/4 cup grated onion
> 1 cup finely diced celery
> 1 red bell pepper, finely diced
> 6 slices bacon, crisp-cooked and crumbled
> Salt and freshly ground black pepper
> 3 T. chopped fresh parsley

Cook the potatoes in a large saucepan of lightly-salted boiling water until tender. Drain in a colander, let cool slightly, then place in a large serving bowl.

Combine the mayonnaise, dill, chiles, and the onion in a small bowl. Stir this mixture into the potatoes. Add the celery, bell pepper, and bacon. Season with salt and pepper to taste. Toss to combine.

Serve warm or refrigerate to serve as a cold potato salad. Garnish with parsley.

 Letting the potato salad chill in the fridge will blend the flavors. Stir before serving.

Burgers, Tacos, and Quesadillas

Black Bean Guacamole Burgers

My favorite burger, with the addition of Hatch chiles.
You can use salsa instead of picante sauce.

2 Hatch green chiles, roasted, peeled,
   stemmed, seeded, and chopped
1 pound lean ground beef
1/2 (15 oz.) can black beans, drained,
   rinsed, and slightly mashed
1/2 cup slightly crushed Fritos
4 whole grain hamburger buns
1/2 cup picante sauce, warmed
1/2 cup chopped onion
4 slices sharp Cheddar cheese
1 cup guacamole

Combine the chiles with the ground beef in a medium-size bowl. Shape into four patties. Grill or broil until done.

While this is cooking, place the beans in a small bowl and warm them in the microwave.

Assemble the burger with a layer of black beans and Fritos on the bottom of the bun, spread the picante sauce and the onion over, place the burger on top of this, place a slice of cheese over the burger, spread the guacamole over, place the top of the bun on, and enjoy.

Hatch Hamburger

This is the first way I enjoyed Hatch chiles. Perfect for a backyard barbecue to celebrate the arrival of Hatch chiles.

1 pound lean ground beef
2 Hatch green chiles, roasted, peeled,
   stemmed, seeded, and chopped
1/4 cup finely chopped onion
2 slices Asadero cheese, cubed
4 hamburger buns or bolillo rolls
4 slices Asadero cheese
1 medium tomato, sliced
1 avocado, peeled, pitted, and sliced

Combine the ground beef, chiles, onion, and cubed cheese in a medium-size bowl. Shape into four patties.

Grill or broil until done. Place each burger on a bun. Top with a slice of cheese, tomato, and avocado.

Use Monterey Jack cheese instead of Asadero. Some people like to also put a slice of Hatch chile on their burger.

Green Chile Burgers

Instead of adding the Hatch chiles to the meat, you can sauté them with some granulated garlic on the stovetop then sprinkle them on the cooked meat before adding the cheese.

1 pound lean ground beef
2 Hatch green chiles, roasted, peeled,
  stemmed, seeded, and chopped
1/2 cup finely chopped onion
1/4 tsp. ground cumin
4 hamburger buns, lightly toasted
  on a grill or under the broiler
1 cup shredded Monterey Jack cheese
4 thick tomato slices
1/2 cup sour cream

Combine the ground beef, chiles, onion, and cumin in a medium-size bowl. Shape into four patties. Grill or broil until done.

Place each burger on a bun. Top with a slice of cheese, tomato, and a dollop of sour cream.

 *To make a **Green Chile Wrap**, shape the mixture into four oblong patties. Grill or broil until done. Serve on warm flour tortillas with avocado slices, sharp Cheddar cheese, and salsa.*

Cheddar Burgers

These burgers are filled with chiles, topped with cheese, and covered with a Hatch chile sauce. It doesn't get much better than this.

>1-1/2 pounds lean ground beef
>7 Hatch green chiles, roasted, peeled,
>   stemmed, seeded, and chopped, divided
>Salt and freshly ground black pepper
>1/2 tsp. ground cumin
>1/2 tsp. paprika
>1/4 tsp. chili powder
>2 T. butter
>1/4 cup chopped onion
>1 garlic clove, minced
>1-1/2 tsp. all-purpose flour
>1/3 cup water
>4 hamburger buns
>4 slices Cheddar cheese

Combine the ground beef, two chiles, the salt and pepper to taste, cumin, paprika, and chili powder in a medium-size bowl. Form into six patties. Grill or broil until done.

While the burgers are cooking, melt the butter in a 12-inch skillet over medium-high heat. Add the onion and sauté until tender. Add the garlic and sauté for one more minute.

Add the flour and cook, stirring, for 2 minutes. Slowly add the water, stirring to combine. Bring to a boil, then reduce the heat and simmer for 2 to 3 minutes. Stir in the remaining chiles and cook until thickened.

Place each burger on a bun, top with a slice of cheese and cover with the chile mixture.

Tex-Mex Turkey Burgers

Turkey burgers offer a lighter alternative to beef and are filled with chopped veggies. Instead of a hamburger bun, wrap them in a Romaine lettuce leaf, like a taco or a burrito. Another choice is to cook them in a skillet, sloppy joe style.

1 (8 oz.) package sliced
   mushrooms, finely chopped
3/4 cup chopped zucchini
1/2 cup finely chopped onion
1/2 cup finely chopped red bell pepper
2 Hatch green chiles, roasted, peeled,
   stemmed, seeded, and chopped
1-1/4 pounds lean ground turkey
1-1/2 T. taco seasoning
6 slices Cheddar cheese
6 hamburger buns
1/3 cup salsa
6 romaine lettuce leaves, chopped

Combine the mushrooms, zucchini, onion, bell pepper, chiles, turkey, and taco seasoning in a medium-size bowl. Shape into six patties.

Grill the burgers over medium coals or cook under a broiler for 6 minutes on each side or until the burgers are cooked through.

Place a slice of cheese over each burger and cook for one more minute, just until the cheese is melted. Place each burger on a bun and top with salsa and lettuce.

 You can also cook the burgers in a 12-inch skillet coated with nonstick cooking spray over medium heat for about 5 minutes per side.

Queso Turkey Burgers

Turkey burgers topped with chiles and queso.

  1 pound lean ground turkey
  2 T. paprika
  2 T. cayenne pepper
  3 T. garlic powder
  Salt and freshly ground black pepper
  1 T. unsalted butter
  1 T. all-purpose flour
  1 cup milk
  1 cup shredded Cheddar cheese
  1 cup shredded Pepper Jack cheese
  4 hamburger buns
  4 Hatch green chiles, roasted, peeled,
      stemmed, seeded, and sliced

Combine the turkey, paprika, cayenne pepper, garlic powder, and the salt and pepper to taste in a medium-size bowl. Shape into four patties. Grill or broil until done.

While the burgers are cooking, make the queso (cheese sauce). Melt the butter in a 12-inch skillet over medium heat. Add the flour, stirring constantly to combine.

Add the milk and whisk constantly until the mixture begins to thicken. Remove the pan from the heat and stir in the Cheddar and Pepper Jack cheeses until melted.

Place each burger on a bun, top with chiles, and smother with the queso.

Cooking equal amounts of butter and flour over heat while stirring constantly creates a roux which thickens the sauce. The roux should be light brown in color and have the texture of sand with a slightly nutty aroma.

Sloppy Joes

Sloppy, but oh so good!

1 pound lean ground beef
1 small onion, chopped
2 garlic cloves, minced
3 Hatch green chiles, roasted, peeled,
  stemmed, seeded, and chopped
3/4 cup ketchup
1/2 cup water
1 T. brown sugar
1 tsp. chili powder
1/2 tsp. dry mustard
1/2 tsp. crushed red pepper flakes
1-1/2 T. tomato paste
4 hamburger buns
Tortilla chips

Brown the ground beef with the onion in a 12-inch skillet over medium-high heat.

Add the garlic and chiles. Cook for one more minute.

Stir in the ketchup, water, brown sugar, chili powder, dry mustard, red pepper flakes, and tomato paste. Bring to a boil, then reduce the heat and simmer for 15 minutes, stirring occasionally.

Spoon equal amounts of the mixture into hamburger buns. Serve with tortilla chips.

 *Use hoagie rolls instead of hamburger buns. For an extra kick, add Worcestershire sauce or hot sauce, such as Tabasco. For **Cheesy Sloppy Joes**, top with shredded Cheddar or Monterey Jack cheese.*

Chicken Black Bean Torta

Tortas are traditionally made with bolillos, *a plain, crisp, white roll that has the doughy filling pulled out before adding the sandwich ingredients. If you are unable to find bolillos, use small, crisp French rolls or sub rolls. Pull out the bready dough inside and stuff the rolls with this recipe.*

2 T. butter
4 bolillos, cut in half lengthwise, excess
    dough removed from both halves
1 cup refried black beans
8 T. shredded Mexican Blend cheese
1 large skinless, boneless chicken breast,
    pounded to 1/8-inch thickness and
    cut into 4 thin slices crosswise
2 Hatch green chiles, roasted, peeled,
    stemmed, seeded, and chopped

Preheat the broiler. Lightly butter the outside of the bolillos. Toast under the broiler for 3 minutes or until golden.

Spread the inside of both halves with the beans, sprinkle with cheese, and cover with aluminum foil to keep warm.

Lightly spray a 12-inch skillet with nonstick cooking spray. Heat over high heat. Add the chicken and sauté for 3 minutes on each side or until cooked through. Place the chicken on top of the bean and cheese mixture. Top with the chiles and toast under the broiler for one more minute. Put both halves of the torta together.

Pork Torta

The essential ingredients in a torta are refried beans and chiles. After that, it's up to your imagination and your taste buds. Cooked pork roast is called for in this recipe but you can substitute chicken, turkey, roast beef, or ham instead of pork.

> 2/3 cup refried beans
> 4 bolillos or sub rolls, cut in half lengthwise,
>   excess dough removed from both halves
> 2 slices cooked roast pork, cut into thin strips
> 2 Hatch green chiles, roasted, peeled,
>   stemmed, seeded, and chopped
> 1 medium tomato, sliced
> 4 slices Cheddar cheese
> 4 T. chopped cilantro
> 4 T. sour cream
> 1 cup chopped lettuce, tossed lightly with olive oil

Preheat the oven to 350 degrees.

Spread the beans on the bottom of half the rolls. Put the pork on top of the beans. Top with the chiles and tomato.

Add the cheese and sprinkle with cilantro. Place the tops of the rolls on the torta.

Wrap each torta in aluminum foil. Place in the oven and bake for 5 to 10 minutes or until heated through.

Remove from the oven and open the rolls. Add the sour cream and lettuce. Put the torta back together.

 Add some cucumber slices, green bell pepper slices, and/or chopped black olives.

Steak 'n' Chile Cheese Subs

Reminiscent of the well-known Philly Cheese Steak Sandwich, this variation offers Hatch chiles instead of green bell peppers.

1 T. vegetable oil

1 medium onion, chopped

4 Hatch green chiles, roasted, peeled, stemmed, seeded, and chopped

2 tsp. garlic salt

3 tsp. dried oregano

1 pound round steak, cut into thin slices

Juice of 1/2 lemon

4 sub or hoagie rolls

1/2 cup shredded Monterey Jack cheese

Heat the oil in a 12-inch skillet over medium-high heat. Add the onion, chiles, garlic salt, and oregano. Sauté until tender. Remove and set aside.

Add the steak, in batches, to the skillet and stir-fry for 2 to 3 minutes, adding more oil if necessary.

Preheat the broiler. Return the vegetables to the skillet. Add the lemon juice, stir, and turn off the heat.

Cut the rolls in half and toast them under the broiler for 5 minutes or until lightly toasted. Remove from the oven and pile on the steak, onion, and chiles. Top with the cheese and return to the oven to melt the cheese.

Add some chopped tomatoes or salsa on top of the sandwich.

Baked Chicken Burritos

These burritos are baked, enchilada style.

2 T. olive oil
2 skinless, boneless chicken
   breasts, cut into bite-size pieces
1/2 red bell pepper, chopped
2 T. chopped onion
1 tsp. chopped garlic
2 Hatch green chiles, roasted, peeled,
   stemmed, seeded, and chopped
1/2 tsp. dried cilantro
1/2 tsp. dried basil
1/4 tsp. ground cumin
1 small tomato, diced
1/4 cup shredded Cheddar cheese
4 (10-inch) flour tortillas, warmed

Preheat the oven to 350 degrees. Lightly spray a 13 x 9 glass baking dish with nonstick cooking spray. Set aside.

Heat the oil in a 12-inch skillet over medium-high heat. Add the chicken, bell pepper, onion, garlic, chiles, cilantro, basil, and cumin. Cook for 10 minutes, stirring occasionally, or until the chicken is cooked through and the vegetables are tender. Add the tomato and cheese. Heat through.

Spoon equal amounts of the filling in the center of each tortilla. Fold in the sides and roll up tightly. Place seam side down in the prepared baking dish. Bake for 15 minutes or until heated through.

For **Baked Pork Burritos,** *substitute 1/2 pound pork tenderloin for the chicken and use a green bell pepper instead of the red bell pepper.*

Chicken and Bean Burritos

Burritos are typically made with large flour tortillas. The ends are folded in and then rolled. Some people like to butter the outside and grill them, panini-style, or place them under the broiler to crisp the burrito.

2 T. olive oil
2 skinless, boneless chicken breasts,
   cut into bite-size pieces
1 tsp. ground cumin
1 tsp. garlic powder
1 (15 oz.) can black beans, drained and rinsed,
   or substitute kidney beans or pinto beans
1 cup fresh or frozen corn, thawed
1/2 cup thick and chunky salsa
2 Hatch green chiles, roasted, peeled,
   stemmed, seeded, and chopped
8 (10-inch) flour tortillas
1/2 cup shredded Cheddar cheese
Sour cream

Heat the oil in a 12-inch skillet over medium-high heat. Add the chicken and brown it on all sides.

Add the cumin, garlic powder, beans, corn, salsa, and chiles. Cook for 10 minutes, stirring occasionally, or until the chicken is cooked through and the vegetables are tender.

Warm the tortillas in the microwave for 30 to 45 seconds to make them soft and pliable. This will prevent them from tearing and make it easier to roll them.

Spoon equal amounts of the filling in the center of each tortilla. Top with cheese. Fold in the sides and roll up tightly.

Serve with sour cream on the side.

Shredded Beef Burritos

Serve with salsa and a side of refried beans.

1 pound boneless chuck steak
1 medium onion, coarsely chopped
4 garlic cloves, chopped
Salt and freshly ground black pepper
6 (10-inch) flour tortillas
1 large tomato, chopped
3 Hatch green chiles, roasted, peeled,
    stemmed, seeded, and chopped
1 (8 oz.) container sour cream
1 (8 oz.) package shredded Monterey
    Jack or Cheddar cheese

Place the beef, onion, and garlic in a medium-size saucepan. Cover with water. Bring to a boil, then reduce the heat and simmer for one hour. Remove the beef to a cutting board, let cool slightly, then shred it with two forks. Season with salt and pepper to taste.

Warm the tortillas in the microwave or in a dry skillet. Place equal amounts of the beef, tomato, chiles, sour cream, and cheese in the center of each tortilla. Fold in the sides and roll up tightly. Serve with salsa and refried beans, if using.

 To make **Beef, Bean, and Cheese Burritos,** *spread warmed refried beans on the tortilla, then layer on the remaining ingredients.*

Shredded Chicken Tacos

The best thing about tacos is all the toppings you can add.

2 T. butter
1/2 cup chopped onion
2 cups shredded, cooked chicken
4 Hatch green chiles, roasted, peeled,
    stemmed, seeded, and chopped
1 (1.25 oz.) package taco seasoning mix
1/4 cup water
12 taco shells
1 cup shredded Monterey Jack cheese
1 (8 oz.) container sour cream
1 avocado, peeled, pitted, and mashed
2 green onions, sliced
1/4 cup chopped black olives
1 large tomato, chopped
2 cups chopped lettuce

Melt the butter in a 12-inch skillet over medium heat.
Add the onion and sauté until tender. Stir in the chicken,
chiles, taco seasoning, and water. Reduce the heat and
simmer for 10 to 15 minutes, stirring occasionally.

While this is cooking, preheat the oven to 250 degrees.
Place the taco shells in the oven on the center rack and warm
them for 10 minutes.

Spoon the chicken mixture into the taco shells. Top with
the cheese, sour cream, avocado, onions, olives, tomato, and
lettuce.

*Instead of serving this in a taco shell or a soft
flour tortilla, serve it open-face on a crisp corn
tortilla for a* **Shredded Chicken Tostada.**

Chile Tacos

I created these one night when I was supposed to be making chili, but had no tomato sauce, so I wrapped them up in a warm flour tortilla and topped them off with a dollop of sour cream.

1 pound lean ground beef
1 medium onion, chopped
4 to 5 T. chili powder
4 to 5 T. ground cumin
2 Hatch green chiles, roasted, peeled,
    stemmed, seeded, and chopped
2 to 3 T. water
6 (8-inch) flour tortillas, warmed
1/2 cup sour cream

Brown the ground beef with the onion in a 12-inch skillet over medium-high heat. Season with the chili powder and cumin while the meat is cooking.

Stir in the chiles. Add enough water to make the meat a little juicy. Heat through.

Spoon the mixture into warm flour tortillas, top with a dollop of sour cream, and fold in half .

Baked Chicken Tacos

Baked, or grilled, tacos are sometimes called Garnachas.
*They're typically made with a corn tortilla which is filled with
a chicken or beef mixture, then lightly grilled and smothered
with Monterey Jack cheese.*

2 T. olive oil
3 skinless, boneless chicken
    breasts, cut into one-inch cubes
1 medium onion, chopped
3 Hatch green chiles, roasted, peeled,
    stemmed, seeded, and chopped
2 (14.5 oz.) cans diced tomatoes
2 tsp. chili powder
1 tsp. ground cumin
1/2 tsp. salt
1/2 tsp. garlic powder
1/2 tsp. dried oregano
1/4 tsp. ground coriander
10 (8-inch) flour tortillas
3-1/2 cups shredded Queso Blanco cheese

Heat the oil in a 12-inch skillet over high heat. Add the
chicken and brown it on all sides. Remove and set aside.

Reduce the heat to medium-high. Add the onion and chiles.
Sauté until the onion is tender.

Stir in the tomatoes, chili powder, cumin, salt, garlic powder,
oregano, and coriander. Cook, stirring occasionally, for 15 minutes
or until the mixture becomes very thick.

Stir in the chicken, reduce the heat to medium-low and simmer
for 5 minutes, stirring occasionally

Preheat the oven to 450 degrees. Warm the tortillas in the
microwave for 30 to 45 seconds to make them soft and pliable.

Spoon equal amounts of the chicken mixture in the center
of each tortilla and roll up. Place seam side down in a 13 x 9
glass baking dish. Bake for 15 minutes or until the tortillas are
crisp and brown.

Remove from the oven and sprinkle with the cheese. Return
to the oven and bake for 5 more minutes to melt the cheese.

*Queso Blanco is a white Mexican cheese similar to
Monterey Jack cheese. It's sold in grocery stores
and Mexican markets.*

Quickie Cheese Quesadillas

Totally quick and easy.

4 (8-inch) flour tortillas
1 (8 oz.) package shredded Colby Jack cheese
2 Hatch green chiles, roasted, peeled,
   stemmed, seeded, and chopped

Heat a 12-inch skillet over medium heat. Place one tortilla
in the skillet and brown it on the bottom, about one minute. Flip
the tortilla over and then sprinkle with the cheese and chiles. Cook
for one minute, then fold the tortilla in half, remove to a plate, cut
into thirds and keep warm. Repeat with the remaining tortillas.

Corn and Beef Tacos

The basic ingredients in this recipe combine to make a flavorful taco. This mixture is also referred to as a picadillo *and tastes great as a filling for gorditas.*

1 pound lean ground beef
1 (15 oz.) can corn, drained
2 Hatch green chiles, roasted, peeled,
    stemmed, seeded, and chopped
1 (8 oz.) can tomato sauce
1/2 cup water
Salt, to taste
1/2 tsp. garlic powder
1 tsp. ground cumin
8 (6-inch) corn tortillas

Brown the ground beef in a 12-inch skillet over medium-high heat.

Stir in the corn, chiles, tomato sauce, water, salt, garlic powder, and cumin. Bring to a boil, then reduce the heat and simmer for 15 minutes or until the sauce has thickened, stirring occasionally.

Warm the tortillas in the microwave or in a dry skillet to make them soft and pliable. Spoon the mixture into the tortillas and fold in half.

Terrific Tacos

There are infinite variations on tacos. They can be made with soft flour tortillas, corn tortillas, or crunchy taco shells. They can be folded, rolled, or wrapped. The main ingredients are seasoned hamburger, pork, chicken, or chorizo sausage and shredded cheese, lettuce, and tomatoes.

1 pound lean ground beef
1/2 cup chopped onion
2 garlic cloves, minced
2 Hatch green chiles, roasted, peeled,
    stemmed, seeded, and chopped
1 T. chili powder
1/2 cup salsa
8 taco shells, warmed
1 cup shredded Cheddar cheese
1 (8 oz.) container sour cream
1 cup chopped lettuce
1 medium tomato, chopped
1 avocado, peeled, pitted, and diced

Brown the ground beef with the onion, garlic, chiles, and chili powder in a 12-inch skillet over medium heat.

Add the salsa. Bring to a boil, stirring constantly. Spoon equal amounts of the ground beef-salsa mixture into each warmed taco shell.

Top with cheese, sour cream, lettuce, tomato, and avocado.

You can add a multitude of other ingredients to your taco... refried beans, green onions, red and/or green bell peppers, cabbage, chopped poblano, jalapeño, or serrano peppers, black olives, corn, salsa, guacamole, and sour cream. The possibilities are endless.

Steak and Corn Tacos, Family-Style

This meal is served family style. If you have a large family or are feeding lots of friends, double or triple this recipe.

>2 T. olive oil
>1 medium red onion, sliced
>1 red bell pepper, cut into strips
>1 green bell pepper, cut into strips
>1/2 pound round steak, cut into
>   1/4-inch thick strips
>3/4 cup frozen whole kernel corn,
>   cooked and drained
>2 Hatch green chiles, roasted, peeled,
>   stemmed, seeded, and chopped
>1/2 tsp. ground cumin
>1/2 tsp. chili powder
>1-1/2 T. minced cilantro
>Salt and freshly ground black pepper
>8 (8-inch) flour tortillas
>1 cup shredded Cheddar cheese
>2 medium tomatoes, chopped
>1 (8 oz.) container sour cream

Heat the oil in a 12-inch skillet over medium heat. Add the onion and both bell peppers. Sauté until tender. Remove to a plate and set aside.

Increase the heat to high. Add the steak to the skillet and stir for one minute or until it is no longer pink.

Return the onion and bell peppers to the skillet. Add the corn, chiles, cumin, and chili powder. Stir until heated through.

Add the cilantro. Season with salt and pepper to taste. Remove the mixture to a platter and keep warm.

Heat a separate 10-inch skillet over medium-high heat. Add the tortillas, one at a time, and cook on both sides. Or warm them in the microwave for 30 to 45 seconds. Place in a tortilla warmer.

Place the cheese, tomatoes, and sour cream in separate bowls. Assemble the tacos and enjoy.

Top Tostadas

A tostada is an open-face sandwich, served on a crisp corn tortilla. In lieu of frying the tortillas, spray them on both sides with nonstick cooking spray and bake them in the oven. This is a quick and easy tostada with toppings.

> 1 (16 oz.) can refried beans, warmed
> 4 (6-inch) corn tortillas, crisply fried
> 1 cup shredded Cheddar cheese
> 1 cup shredded, seasoned cooked
>   beef, chicken, or pork
> 2 Hatch green chiles, roasted, peeled,
>   stemmed, seeded, and chopped
> 1 cup chopped lettuce
> 1 large tomato, diced
> 1 cup guacamole
> 1/2 cup sour cream
> 1/4 cup sliced black olives

Spread equal amounts of the beans on each tortilla. Sprinkle with cheese and layer on the remaining ingredients.

Chicken Quesadillas

Cheese quesadillas are often served as an appetizer with salsa for dipping. Add some fillings and these quesadillas make a light lunch. Making a quesadilla is similar to making a grilled cheese sandwich.

4 (8-inch) flour tortillas
1-1/2 cups shredded Mexican Blend cheese
2 Hatch green chiles, roasted, peeled,
   stemmed, seeded, and chopped
1 cup shredded, cooked chicken
1 small tomato, seeded and chopped
3 T. finely chopped green onion
1 T. chopped cilantro
Salsa
Sour cream

Heat a 10-inch nonstick skillet or comal over medium heat. Lay one tortilla in the skillet. Cook for one minute or until the tortilla is soft and pliable, and is lightly browned on the bottom. Flip the tortilla over and sprinkle one-fourth of the cheese, chiles, chicken, tomato, onion, and cilantro over the tortilla. Cook for one to 2 minutes.

Fold the tortilla in half, using a spatula. Press down gently with the spatula to keep the fillings inside. Remove it to a plate and keep warm. Repeat with the remaining tortillas.

Cut each quesadilla into thirds. Serve with salsa and sour cream on the side.

Hatch, New Mexico, is the chile capital of the world.

Chicken Chile Quesadillas

Chicken, chiles, and cheese make a great quesadilla.

2 skinless, boneless chicken breasts
2 Hatch green chiles, roasted, peeled,
    stemmed, seeded, and chopped
1/4 cup chopped cilantro
3 green onions, thinly sliced
8 (8-inch) flour tortillas
4 T. butter, melted
1 cup shredded Monterey Jack cheese
1 cup shredded Cheddar cheese

Place the chicken in a large saucepan and cover with water. Bring to a boil, then reduce the heat and simmer for 15 minutes or until the chicken is cooked through. Remove the chicken to a cutting board, let cool slightly, then shred it with two forks.

Preheat the oven to 350 degrees. Combine the chicken, chiles, cilantro, and onions in a large bowl. Set aside.

Brush one side of four tortillas with half the butter. Place the tortillas, buttered side down, on a baking sheet. Brush the tops of the remaining tortillas with the remaining butter and set aside.

Combine the Monterey Jack and Cheddar cheeses in a medium-size bowl.

Spread equal amounts of the chicken mixture and cheese over the tortillas on the baking sheet. Place the remaining tortillas on top, buttered side up. Bake for 5 minutes or until heated through and the cheese is melted. Cut each quesadilla into four wedges.

Use ground beef or shredded pork instead of chicken. Add refried beans. Serve with salsa and/or sour cream.

Chicken Fajita Quesadillas

This recipe calls for sautéing the onion and peppers, but you can grill them with the chicken instead of sautéing them.

4 skinless, boneless chicken breasts
4 T. olive oil, divided
1 (1.25 oz.) package taco seasoning mix, divided
2 Hatch green chiles, roasted, peeled,
   stemmed, seeded, and chopped
1 red bell pepper, cut into strips
1 yellow bell pepper, cut into strips
1 red onion, thinly sliced
1 tsp. minced garlic
1 (8 oz.) package cream cheese, softened
1-1/2 cups shredded Mexican Blend cheese
12 (8-inch) flour tortillas
1 T. chopped cilantro
Salsa and sour cream

Brush both sides of the chicken with 2 T. of the oil. Sprinkle with some of the taco seasoning. Grill until done. Remove to a cutting board, let cool slightly, then cut into strips. Set aside.

Preheat the oven to 400 degrees.

Heat the remaining oil in a 12-inch skillet over medium heat. Add the chiles, red and yellow bell peppers, and onion. Sauté until tender. Add the garlic and sauté for one more minute. Remove the pan from the heat and set aside.

Combine the cream cheese, the Mexican Blend cheese, and 1 T. of the taco seasoning in a medium-size bowl. Set aside.

Place six tortillas on a large baking sheet. Spread the cream cheese mixture on each tortilla. Top with the chicken strips and bell pepper mixture. Sprinkle with the remaining taco seasoning and the cilantro, then cover with the remaining tortillas.

Cover loosely with aluminum foil and bake for 10 minutes or until heated through. Cut each quesadilla into four wedges. Serve with salsa and sour cream.

Baked Beef Quesadillas

Baked in the oven instead of cooked on the stove, these quesadillas crisp up nicely.

1 pound lean ground beef
1 small onion, chopped
3/4 cup salsa
2 Hatch green chiles, roasted, peeled,
    stemmed, seeded, and chopped
2 cups shredded Colby Jack cheese
10 (8-inch) flour tortillas, warmed

Preheat the oven to 450 degrees. Lightly spray a baking sheet with nonstick cooking spray.

Brown the ground beef with the onion in a 12-inch skillet over medium-high heat. Add the salsa, chiles, and cheese. Stir until the cheese melts.

Place half the tortillas on the prepared baking sheet. Spoon equal amounts of the beef mixture on each tortilla. Place the remaining tortillas on top. Lightly spray the tops with nonstick cooking spray. Bake for 8 to 10 minutes or until the tortillas are lightly brown. Cut each quesadilla into four wedges.

Cheesy Quesadillas

*These are made with Cheddar and Monterey Jack cheeses.
Hatch chiles and bacon are tucked inside.*

4 T. butter, softened
4 (8-inch) flour tortillas
1/2 cup shredded Monterey Jack cheese
1/2 cup shredded Cheddar cheese
1 small tomato, chopped
4 tsp. diced onion
2 T. Hatch green chiles, roasted, peeled,
    stemmed, seeded, and chopped
1 strip bacon, crisp-cooked and crumbled
1/2 tsp. finely chopped cilantro
Sour cream, guacamole, and/or salsa

Heat a comal or a 12-inch skillet over medium heat.

Spread the butter on one side of each tortilla. Place one tortilla, buttered-side down, in the skillet. Sprinkle the Monterey Jack and Cheddar cheeses evenly over the tortilla, leaving room at the edges so the filling doesn't spill out. Sprinkle the tomato, onion, chiles, bacon, and cilantro evenly over the cheese.

Top with another tortilla, buttered side up. When the bottom has browned, about one minute, flip it over and brown the other side for one minute. Remove to a plate and keep warm. Repeat with the remaining tortillas.

Cut each quesadilla into four wedges. Serve with sour cream, guacamole, and /or salsa for dipping.

*This recipe doubles, or triples, easily in case you're
hungry or are feeding a crowd.*

Quickie Quesadillas

These baked quesadillas take ten to fifteen minutes from beginning to end and are layered with flavor.

8 (8-inch) flour tortillas
2 cups shredded, cooked chicken
3/4 cup taco sauce
1 (16 oz.) can refried beans
2 Hatch green chiles, roasted, peeled, stemmed, seeded, and chopped
1 avocado, peeled, pitted, and chopped
1/2 cup shredded Monterey Jack cheese
1/2 cup shredded Cheddar cheese
2 green onions, sliced
Sour cream

Preheat the oven to 400 degrees.

Lightly spray both sides of each tortilla with nonstick cooking spray. Place the tortillas on a baking sheet. Bake for 3 minutes or until the tortillas are lightly toasted.

Mix the chicken with the taco sauce in a medium-size bowl.

Remove the tortillas from the oven. Spread the beans on four tortillas. Top with the chicken mixture. Sprinkle the chiles, avocado, Monterey Jack and Cheddar cheeses, and onions over the chicken mixture. Top with the remaining four tortillas.

Return to the oven and bake for 5 minutes or until heated through and the cheese is melted. Cut each quesadilla into four wedges. Serve with sour cream.

 You can buy cooked, shredded chicken at the grocery store in the refrigerated section or use a rotisserie chicken for this recipe. Remove the skin and shred.

Shrimp Quesadillas

While this recipe calls for shrimp, you can use any kind of firm fish to create a fish quesadilla.

2 T. butter
1 cup frozen corn, thawed
1/2 cup chopped onion
2 garlic cloves, minced
2 Hatch green chiles, roasted, peeled,
   stemmed, seeded, and chopped
2 medium tomatoes, chopped
1 pound shrimp, deveined and chopped
1 T. fresh lime juice
4 T. chopped cilantro
Salt and freshly ground black pepper
8 (8-inch) flour tortillas
1-1/2 cups shredded Asadero cheese
Sour cream
1 lime, cut into wedges

Melt the butter in a 12-inch skillet over medium heat. Add the corn and onion. Sauté until tender. Add the garlic and sauté for one more minute. Add the chiles and tomatoes. Cook for 3 minutes. Add the shrimp and cook until opaque. Sprinkle in the lime juice and cilantro. Season with salt and pepper to taste. Remove the pan from the heat.

Heat a separate 12-inch skillet over medium heat. Place one tortilla in the skillet. Sprinkle equal amounts of the shrimp mixture and a little cheese evenly over the tortilla. Top with another tortilla. Cook for 2 to 3 minutes per side, pressing down with a spatula until the cheese melts and the tortilla is golden brown. Remove to a plate and keep warm. Repeat with the remaining tortillas. Cut each into four wedges. Serve with sour cream and a lime wedge.

Chile Chili

Chile Colorado

This chili has no beans—just meat, tomatoes, and chiles.

2 tsp. vegetable oil
1-1/2 pounds round steak, cut into cubes
6 Hatch green chiles, roasted, peeled,
   stemmed, seeded, and chopped
1 tsp. salt
2 (14.5 oz.) cans crushed tomatoes
1 garlic clove, minced
Flour tortillas, warmed
Sour cream

Heat the oil in a large saucepan over medium-high heat. Add the steak and brown it on all sides. Remove the meat to a plate and set aside.

Add the chiles, salt, tomatoes, and garlic. Bring to a boil, then reduce the heat and simmer for 5 minutes.

Return the meat to the pan, along with any accumulated juices. Stir to mix. Bring to a boil again, then reduce the heat, cover, and simmer for one hour, stirring occasionally.

Serve with warm flour tortillas and sour cream.

 *To make **Chile Verde Colorado**, use one pound tomatillos, rinsed, husked, cored, and chopped instead of the tomatoes.*

Corn Chip Chili

The crushed Fritos add a nice crunch to this chili.

1-1/2 pounds lean ground beef
1 medium onion, finely chopped
1 (16 oz.) can tomato or V-8 juice
1 (14.5 oz.) can Mexican stewed
   tomatoes, cut up
2 (15.5 oz.) cans dark red kidney
   beans, drained and rinsed
3 T. chili powder, or more to taste
3/4 tsp. ground cumin
1 tsp. garlic powder
2 Hatch green chiles, roasted, peeled,
   stemmed, seeded, and chopped
1-1/2 cups crushed Fritos
1 cup shredded Mexican Blend cheese

Brown the ground beef with the onion in a large saucepan over medium-high heat.

Stir in the tomato juice, tomatoes, beans, chili powder, cumin, garlic powder, and chiles. Bring to a boil, then reduce the heat, cover, and simmer for one hour, stirring occasionally.

Ladle into individual serving bowls. Top with the Fritos and cheese.

Beer 'n' Black Bean Chili

A tall glass of cold beer goes great with chili. It's even better if you actually put the beer in the chili.

    2 T. olive oil
    2 pounds stew beef cubes
    2 cups chopped onion
    4 Hatch green chiles, roasted, peeled,
        stemmed, seeded, and chopped
    1 (14.5 oz.) can beef broth
    1 cup beer (Dos Equis is preferred)
    1 (6 oz.) can tomato paste
    3 T. chili powder
    1 tsp. garlic powder
    1 tsp. dried oregano
    1/2 tsp. ground cumin
    1/2 tsp. salt
    2 (15 oz.) cans black beans,
        drained and rinsed
    1 cup shredded Cheddar cheese
    White tortilla chips

Heat the oil in a large saucepan over medium-high heat. Add the beef and brown it on all sides. Remove to a plate and set aside. Add the onion to the pan and sauté until tender.

Return the meat to the pan, along with any accumulated juices. Stir in the chiles, broth, beer, tomato paste, chili powder, garlic powder, oregano, cumin, and salt. Bring to a boil, then reduce the heat and simmer for one hour, stirring occasionally.

Add the beans and simmer for 20 more minutes, stirring occasionally.

Ladle into individual serving bowls. Sprinkle with the cheese. Serve with tortilla chips.

Picante Corn Chili

The addition of corn to this chili adds color and texture.

1-1/2 pounds lean ground beef
1 medium onion, finely chopped
1 garlic clove, minced
1 (14.5 oz.) can diced tomatoes
1/2 cup picante sauce
1 (8 oz.) can whole kernel corn, drained
4 Hatch green chiles, roasted, peeled,
    stemmed, seeded, and chopped
2 (15.5 oz.) cans pinto beans, drained and rinsed
1/2 tsp. ground cumin
1 cup water
1/2 cup shredded Monterey Jack cheese
1/2 cup shredded Cheddar cheese
1/4 cup chopped green onion
Tortilla chips

Brown the ground beef with the onion and garlic in a large saucepan over medium heat.

Stir in the tomatoes, picante sauce, corn, chiles, beans, cumin, and water. Bring to a boil, then reduce the heat, cover, and simmer for 20 minutes, stirring occasionally.

Ladle into individual serving bowls. Top with the Monterey Jack and Cheddar cheeses and the onion. Serve with tortilla chips.

Hatch green chiles come in heat levels from mild to medium, and from hot to extra-hot. You can't tell the heat level from looks; you have to bite into it to find out how hot, or not, it is.

Crock Pot Chili

Cooked in a crock pot, this chili develops a lot of flavor and is a convenient meal for a busy day. Cook the meat first in a skillet, then add it, with all the remaining ingredients, to a crock pot.

1 pound lean ground beef
3/4 cup chopped celery
1 small onion, chopped
1 green bell pepper, chopped
1 (14.5 oz.) can diced tomatoes
1 (8 oz.) can tomato sauce
2 T. tomato paste
1 (15.5 oz.) can dark red kidney
   beans, drained and rinsed
2 Hatch green chiles, roasted, peeled,
   stemmed, seeded, and chopped
1 T. chili powder, or more to taste
1/4 tsp. garlic powder
1 cup shredded Cheddar cheese
Sour cream
Tortilla chips

Brown the ground beef in a 12-inch skillet over high heat.

Transfer to a crock pot. Add the celery, onion, bell pepper, tomatoes, tomato sauce, tomato paste, beans, chiles, chili powder, and garlic powder. Stir to mix. Cook on high for 4 to 5 hours, or on low for 8 hours. Ladle into individual serving bowls. Top with cheese and a dollop of sour cream. Serve with tortilla chips.

If you prefer, you can cook this on a stove. Let it simmer for 2 to 3 hours, stirring occasionally.

Chile Chili

Chili is usually cooked with beef, beans, and peppers in a tomato-based sauce, though there's a hot debate about whether true chili should have beans. Chili is also referred to as a bowl of red.

1 pound lean ground beef
1 pound stew beef cubes
1 green bell pepper, chopped
1 large onion, chopped
4 Hatch green chiles, roasted, peeled,
   stemmed, seeded, and chopped
1 (8 oz.) can tomato sauce
2 (14.5 oz.) cans diced tomatoes
2 (15.5 oz.) cans dark red kidney
   beans, drained and rinsed
3 T. chili powder
1/2 tsp. salt
1/2 tsp. cinnamon
1/2 tsp. ground cumin
1/2 tsp. dried oregano
1/2 tsp. garlic powder
1/4 tsp. black pepper
1/2 cup shredded Cheddar cheese

Brown the ground beef and the stew beef with the bell pepper and onion in a large saucepan over medium-high heat.

Stir in the chiles, tomato sauce, tomatoes, beans, chili powder, salt, cinnamon, cumin, oregano, garlic powder, and pepper. Bring to a boil, then reduce the heat, cover, and simmer for 2 hours or until the stew beef is tender, stirring occasionally.

Ladle into individual serving bowls. Top with cheese.

Slow Simmered Chunky Chili

The longer this cooks, the more flavorful it becomes. Adjust the chili powder and cayenne pepper to suit your taste.

    2 pounds stew beef cubes
    1 large onion, chopped
    2 garlic cloves, chopped
    2 (14.5 oz.) cans diced tomatoes
    2 (8 oz.) cans tomato sauce
    2 (15.5 oz.) cans pinto beans,
        drained and rinsed
    6 Hatch green chiles, roasted, peeled,
        stemmed, seeded, and chopped
    1-1/2 tsp. salt
    3 T. chili powder
    1 T. cayenne pepper
    1 tsp. dried oregano
    Tortilla chips

Heat a large saucepan over medium-high heat. Rinse the meat under cold running water and add it to the pan. Brown the meat in its own juices, adding more water if necessary.

Add the onion. Continue to cook until the onion is tender. Add the garlic and sauté for one more minute.

Stir in the tomatoes, tomato sauce, beans, chiles, salt, chili powder, cayenne pepper, and oregano. Bring to a boil, then reduce the heat and simmer for 2 hours, stirring occasionally. Serve with tortilla chips.

 Add any toppings you'd like... cheese, sour cream, green onions, cilantro, chopped cucumber, and/or chopped avocado.

Tortilla Chili

Adding cut-up corn tortillas to this chili adds flavor and thickens the sauce.

1 pound lean ground beef
1 T. minced garlic
2 Hatch green chiles, roasted, peeled,
    stemmed, seeded, and chopped
1 medium onion, finely chopped
1 (14.5 oz.) can diced tomatoes
1 (6 oz.) can tomato paste
1 cup water, more if necessary
4 T. chili powder, or more to taste
1/4 tsp. celery salt
1/4 tsp. black pepper
2 (6-inch) corn tortillas, cut up
1 (15.5 oz.) can dark red kidney
    beans, drained and rinsed
1 cup shredded Cheddar cheese
Sour cream

Brown the meat with the garlic, chiles, and onion in a large saucepan over medium heat. Stir in the tomatoes, tomato paste, water, chili powder, celery salt, and pepper. Bring to a boil, then reduce the heat, cover, and simmer for 45 to 50 minutes, stirring occasionally. Add the tortillas and beans. Simmer for 15 more minutes, stirring occasionally.

Ladle into individual serving bowls. Top with cheese and a dollop of sour cream.

To make **Chicken Tortilla Chili**, *substitute 2 skinless, boneless chicken breasts, coarsely cut up and browned in 2 T. olive oil for the ground beef. For* **Chicken Salsa Chili**, *use 1 cup salsa instead of the diced tomatoes.*

Beefy Beer Chili

No beans about it. This chili is thick, meaty, spicy, and totally delicious.

1 T. vegetable oil
2 large onions, chopped
1 green bell pepper, chopped
1 stalk celery, chopped
2 garlic cloves, minced
6 Hatch green chiles, roasted, peeled,
   stemmed, seeded, and chopped, divided
4 pounds coarse ground round
8 T. chili powder
1 T. ground cumin
2 tsp. garlic salt
1/4 tsp. Tabasco sauce
1 cup beer
1-1/4 cups water
1 (14.5 oz.) can stewed tomatoes
1 (8 oz.) can tomato sauce
1 (6 oz.) can tomato paste

Heat the oil in a large saucepan over medium heat. Add the onions, bell pepper, celery, garlic, and half the chiles. Sauté until the onion and bell pepper are tender. Remove and set aside. Add the beef to the pan and cook until it is browned.

While the beef is cooking, combine the chili powder, cumin, garlic salt, Tabasco sauce, and the beer in a medium-size bowl. Let stand for 2 minutes.

Stir the beer mixture into the beef and return the vegetable mixture to the pan. Stir in the water, stewed tomatoes, tomato sauce, tomato paste, and the remaining chiles. Bring to a boil, then reduce the heat, cover, and simmer for 3 to 4 hours, stirring occasionally.

Basic Green Chili

Lots of chiles are in this recipe. Adjust the amount to suit your taste. Just remember that the longer it cooks, the spicier it becomes.

>3 T. all-purpose flour
>1/4 tsp. black pepper
>2 pounds pork tenderloin, cut into cubes
>3 T. vegetable oil
>2 cups chopped onion
>20 Hatch green chiles, roasted, peeled, stemmed, seeded, and chopped
>2 garlic cloves, minced
>1 (14.5 oz.) can diced tomatoes
>1 (14 oz.) can chicken broth
>1 cup water
>Flour tortillas, warmed
>Sour cream

Mix the flour and pepper in a plastic Zip-lock bag. Add the pork, seal the bag, and shake to coat the pork.

Heat the oil in a large saucepan over medium-high heat. Add the pork and brown it on all sides. Add the onion, chiles, and garlic. Sauté for one more minute.

Stir in the tomatoes, broth, and water. Bring to a boil, then reduce the heat and simmer for 2 to 3 hours, stirring occasionally.

Serve with warm flour tortillas and sour cream.

For a thicker chili, add more flour. If you'd like it thinner, add more water. You can cook this in a crock pot after browning the meat. If you like beans in your chili, add them during the last half hour of cooking.

Green Salsa Chili

Slow simmered and spicy.

2 T. vegetable oil
2 pounds pork tenderloin, cut into cubes
1 cup coarsely chopped onion
1 (14 oz.) can chicken broth
3 garlic cloves, minced
2-1/2 T. chicken bouillon granules
1 tsp. celery salt
1 T. all-purpose flour
2 tsp. dried oregano
1 T. ground cumin
1 T. chili powder
1 (10 oz.) bottle green salsa
12 Hatch green chiles, roasted, peeled,
    stemmed, seeded, and chopped
Tortilla chips

Heat the oil in a large saucepan over medium-high heat. Add the pork and onion. Cook until the pork is brown on all sides and the onion is tender.

Stir in the broth. Bring to a boil, then reduce the heat and simmer for one hour, stirring occasionally.

Stir in the garlic, bouillon, celery salt, flour, oregano, cumin, chili powder, salsa, and chiles. Simmer for one more hour, stirring occasionally.

Serve with tortilla chips.

If you'd like it spicier, add some Tabasco sauce or other hot sauce.

Del Rio Chili

A combination of pork and beef, along with a serrano pepper and Hatch chiles make this a perfect meal on a cool night.

2 T. olive oil
2 pounds lean pork, cut into cubes
1 pound stew beef cubes
2 cups chopped onion
1 serrano pepper, stemmed,
   seeded, and chopped
2 garlic cloves, minced
1/4 cup chili powder
1 T. ground cumin
2 tsp. dried oregano
2 (14.5 oz.) cans diced tomatoes
1 (14.5 oz.) can beef broth
1 (12 oz.) can beer
2 Hatch green chiles, roasted, peeled,
   stemmed, seeded, and chopped
2 (15.5 oz.) cans pinto beans,
   drained and rinsed
1/2 cup shredded Cheddar cheese
2 T. chopped cilantro
White tortilla chips

Heat the oil in a large saucepan over medium-high heat. Add the pork, beef, and onion. Cook until the meat is brown on all sides and the onion is tender.

Stir in the serrano pepper, garlic, chili powder, cumin, and oregano. Cook for 5 minutes.

Stir in the tomatoes, broth, beer, and chiles. Bring to a boil, then reduce the heat, cover, and simmer for 1-1/2 hours or until the pork and the beef are very tender, stirring occasionally.

Add the beans and cook, uncovered, for 10 more minutes or until the sauce thickens.

Ladle into individual serving bowls. Top with the cheese and sprinkle with cilantro. Tuck a few tortilla chips in around the side of the bowl.

Cayenne Chili

Flavored with cumin and cayenne pepper, and featuring pinto beans, this chili only takes 30 minutes to cook and will warm you from the inside out.

1/2 pound crumbled chorizo sausage
1 medium onion, chopped
1 (14.5 oz.) can beef broth
2 (15.5 oz.) cans pinto beans,
    drained and rinsed
1 (8 oz.) can tomato sauce
4 Hatch green chiles, roasted, peeled,
    stemmed, seeded, and chopped
1 T. chili powder
3 tsp. ground cumin
1/4 tsp. cayenne pepper

Cook the sausage with the onion in a medium-size saucepan over medium-high heat. Drain.

Stir in the broth, beans, tomato sauce, chiles, chili powder, cumin, and cayenne pepper. Bring to a boil, then reduce the heat and simmer for 30 minutes, stirring occasionally.

Chorizo Chili

This chili should come with a warning. It's very spicy and is not for people with timid taste buds. Spread some sour cream on a flour tortilla to cool and soothe your taste buds.

1 pound crumbled chorizo sausage
2 cups chopped onion
2 cups water
1 T. chili powder
1-1/2 tsp. dried oregano
2 tsp. ground cumin
1/4 tsp. crushed red pepper flakes
2 (14.5 oz.) cans stewed tomatoes
1 (15 oz.) can black-eyed peas,
    drained and rinsed
2 Hatch green chiles, roasted, peeled,
    stemmed, seeded, and chopped
2 garlic cloves, minced
1 cup shredded Cheddar cheese
1 cup sour cream
2 green onions, sliced
1 medium tomato, diced
Flour tortillas, warmed
Sour cream

Brown the chorizo with the onion in a large saucepan over medium-high heat. Drain.

Stir in the water, chili powder, oregano, cumin, red pepper flakes, tomatoes, black-eyed peas, chiles, and garlic. Bring to a boil, then reduce the heat and simmer for one hour, stirring occasionally.

Ladle into individual serving bowls. Top with cheese and a dollop of sour cream. Sprinkle with the onions and tomato. Serve with tortillas and sour cream on the side.

Chicken Cannellini Chili

This white bean chili has lots of beans.

1 T. vegetable oil
4 skinless, boneless chicken
   breasts, cut into bite-size pieces
1 medium onion, chopped
2 jalapeño peppers, stemmed,
   seeded, and chopped
1 garlic clove, minced
1 (14 oz.) can chicken broth
2 (15.5 oz.) cans cannellini beans,
   drained and rinsed
1 (15.5 oz.) can cannellini beans,
   drained, rinsed, and mashed
6 Hatch green chiles, roasted, peeled,
   stemmed, seeded, and chopped
1 tsp. ground cumin
1/2 tsp. dried oregano
1/2 tsp. chili powder
1/4 tsp. black pepper
1/8 tsp. cayenne pepper
1/2 cup shredded Monterey Jack cheese
1/2 cup sour cream

Heat the oil in a large saucepan over medium-high heat. Add the chicken and brown it on all sides. Remove and set aside. Add the onion and jalapeños to the pan and sauté until tender. Add the garlic and sauté for one more minute.

Return the chicken to the pan. Stir in the broth, beans, chiles, cumin, oregano, chili powder, black pepper, and cayenne pepper. Bring to a boil, then reduce the heat and simmer for 45 minutes, stirring occasionally. Ladle into individual serving bowls. Top with cheese and a dollop of sour cream.

Chicken Chili

This is a mild-mannered chili. Heat it up with more Hatch chiles.

> 2 T. olive oil, divided
> 1 medium onion, chopped
> 1 green bell pepper, chopped
> 2 skinless, boneless chicken breasts, chopped
> 3 T. chili powder
> 1 tsp. ground cumin
> 1/2 tsp. dried oregano
> 3 garlic cloves, minced
> 1 (15.5 oz.) can dark red kidney
>   beans, drained and rinsed
> 1 (14.5 oz.) can diced tomatoes
> 1 (8 oz.) can tomato sauce
> 4 Hatch green chiles, roasted, peeled,
>   stemmed, seeded, and chopped
> 1 cup shredded Cheddar cheese
> Tortilla chips or cornbread

Heat 1 T. of the oil in a medium-size saucepan over medium heat. Add the onion and bell pepper. Sauté for 5 minutes or until the vegetables are tender. Remove and set aside.

Add the remaining oil to the pan and raise the heat to high. Add the chicken and brown it on all sides.

Return the vegetables to the pan. Stir in the chili powder, cumin, oregano, and garlic.

Stir in the beans, tomatoes, tomato sauce, and chiles. Bring to a boil, then reduce the heat, cover, and simmer for one hour, stirring occasionally.

Ladle into individual serving bowls. Top with cheese. Serve with tortilla chips or cornbread.

Pinto Chicken Chili

Pinto beans are the preferred choice of beans in a bowl of chili.

2 T. olive oil
4 skinless, boneless chicken breasts, cut into cubes
1 large onion, chopped
5 Hatch green chiles, roasted, peeled,
    stemmed, seeded, and chopped
3 garlic cloves, minced
1/4 cup sun-dried tomatoes
2 T. chili powder
1 T. ground cumin
2 tsp. dried oregano
2 cups chicken broth
1 cup dried pinto beans, soaked
    overnight in water, drained
1 large tomato, chopped
1 cup frozen corn, thawed

Heat the oil in a large saucepan over medium heat. Add the chicken and brown it on all sides. Remove and set aside.

Add the onion to the pan and sauté until tender. Add the chiles and garlic. Sauté for one more minute.

Stir in the sun-dried tomatoes, chili powder, cumin, and oregano. Cook for 2 to 3 minutes. Return the chicken to the pan. Stir in the broth and beans. Bring to a boil, then reduce the heat and simmer for one hour, stirring occasionally.

Add the chopped tomato and corn. Simmer for 30 more minutes or until the beans are tender.

The sun-dried tomatoes add a burst of tomatoey goodness and flavor.

White Wine Chicken Chili

Bacon and mushrooms are mixed in with this chili.

4 slices bacon, chopped

2 skinless, boneless chicken breasts,
  coarsely chopped

1 medium onion, chopped

2 garlic cloves, minced

4 Hatch green chiles, roasted, peeled,
  stemmed, seeded, and chopped

2 (14.5 oz.) cans diced tomatoes

1 cup white wine, divided

1 T. dried oregano

2 T. chili powder

1/8 tsp. ground cinnamon

1 (8 oz.) container sliced mushrooms,
  coarsely chopped

Cook the bacon, chicken, and the onion in a medium-size saucepan over medium-high heat until the bacon is crisp, the chicken is cooked through, and the onion is tender. Add the garlic and chiles. Sauté for one more minute. Drain.

Stir in the tomatoes, 1/2 cup of the wine, the oregano, chili powder, and cinnamon. Bring to a boil, then reduce the heat and simmer for 30 minutes, stirring occasionally. Add the remaining wine and the mushrooms. Bring to a low boil and cook for 15 to 20 more minutes or until the liquid is reduced by half.

Tequila Turkey Chili

This is a quick and easy recipe.

1 pound lean ground turkey
1 medium onion, chopped
1 (14 oz.) can chicken broth
4 Hatch green chiles, roasted, peeled,
   stemmed, seeded, and chopped
1 (15 oz.) can black beans, drained and rinsed
1-1/2 tsp. ground cumin
1-1/2 tsp. chili powder
Splash of tequila
1 lime, cut into wedges

Cook the turkey with the onion in a medium-size saucepan over medium heat until the turkey is browned and the onion is tender.

Stir in the broth, chiles, beans, cumin, and chili powder. Bring to a boil, then reduce the heat and simmer for 30 minutes, stirring occasionally.

Add the tequila, stir to mix, and serve with a lime wedge.

Add corn and/or tomatoes. Top the chili with cheese or sour cream. Serve with tortilla chips.

Chile Turkey Chili

This is the perfect chili to make on a cold, rainy night.

1 pound lean ground turkey
1 medium onion, chopped
1 T. ground cumin, divided
3 T. chili powder, divided
1 T. fajita seasoning, divided
2 garlic cloves, minced
2 Hatch green chiles, roasted, peeled,
  stemmed, seeded, and chopped
1 (8 oz.) can tomato sauce
1 (14.5 oz.) can diced tomatoes
1 (15.5 oz.) can dark red kidney
  beans, drained and rinsed
1 (11 oz.) can Mexicorn, drained
1 cup shredded Cheddar cheese
Cornbread and butter

Cook the turkey with the onion in a medium-size saucepan over medium-high heat until the turkey is nearly browned and the onion is tender. Season with half the cumin, chili powder, and fajita seasoning while the meat is cooking.

Stir in the garlic and chiles. Season with the remaining cumin, chili powder, and fajita seasoning. Cook for 5 more minutes or until the meat is browned. Stir in the tomato sauce, tomatoes, beans, and Mexicorn. Bring to a boil, then reduce the heat, cover, and simmer for one hour, stirring occasionally.

Top with cheese. Serve with warm cornbread and butter.

 Mexicorn is canned sweet corn with red and green bell peppers.

Enchiladas

Beef Enchiladas with Sour Cream Sauce

The sour cream sauce is heavenly.

1 pound lean ground beef
3/4 cup chopped onion
5 Hatch green chiles, roasted, peeled,
     stemmed, seeded, and chopped, divided
4 tsp. butter
1/4 cup all-purpose flour
2 cups chicken broth, heated
1 (8 oz.) container sour cream
12 (6-inch) corn tortillas, softened
1 cup shredded Monterey Jack cheese, divided

Preheat the oven to 425 degrees. Lightly spray a 13 x 9 glass baking dish with nonstick cooking spray. Set aside.

Brown the ground beef with the onion and two of the chiles in a 12-inch skillet over medium-high heat.

While this is cooking, melt the butter in a medium-size saucepan over medium heat. Add the flour and stir constantly to make a roux. Add the hot chicken broth and whisk until thickened. When the mixture is thickened, add the remaining chiles and the sour cream. Remove the pan from the heat and whisk constantly to prevent the sour cream from separating.

Add a spoonful or two of the sour cream sauce to the beef mixture to moisten it.

Spoon equal amounts of the meat mixture in the center of each tortilla. Sprinkle with half the cheese. Roll up and place seam side down in the prepared baking dish.

Pour the remaining sour cream sauce over. Sprinkle with the remaining cheese. Bake for 15 to 20 minutes or until the cheese begins to brown.

Beef and Cream Cheese Enchiladas

I made these one night when I was craving enchiladas. They were absolutely delicious. I used Hatch enchilada sauce; if you can't find it, use a good enchilada sauce.

> 1 pound lean ground beef
> 1/2 medium onion, finely diced
> 1/4 tsp. black pepper
> 1/4 tsp. ground cumin
> 1/4 tsp. chili powder
> 1 garlic clove, finely diced
> 3 Hatch green chiles, roasted, peeled,
>   stemmed, seeded, and chopped
> 1 (14 oz.) can Hatch enchilada sauce, divided
> 10 (6-inch) white corn tortillas, softened
> 1 (8 oz.) brick Colby Jack cheese, cut into 20 logs
> 1 (8 oz.) package cream cheese, cut into 10 logs
> 1 (8 oz.) package shredded Colby Jack cheese

Brown the ground beef with the onion in a 12-inch skillet over medium-high heat. Season with the pepper, cumin, and chili powder while the beef is cooking.

Add the garlic and chiles. Cook for one more minute. Add a spoonful or two of the enchilada sauce into the meat mixture to moisten it a bit. Take the pan off the heat.

While this is cooking, preheat the oven to 350 degrees. Pour 1/4 cup of the enchilada sauce into the bottom of a 13 x 9 glass baking dish.

Lay one softened tortilla in the sauce in the baking dish. Add two logs of Colby Jack, one cream cheese log (stretch it to fit over the cheese logs), and a heaping spoonful or two of the meat mixture. Roll it up (your hands are going to get very messy with the sauce, but that's part of the joy of making enchiladas). When you're done rolling, it should already be seam side down, so just push it to the end of the baking dish and repeat nine more times. You may have to add more sauce to the baking dish to coat the tortillas as you roll them. You should end up with eight in a row and two on the side.

Pour the remaining enchilada sauce over the tortillas. Smother them with the shredded cheese, cover with aluminum foil, and bake for 35 to 40 minutes. Remove from the oven and uncover. Return to the oven and bake for 10 more minutes or until the cheese begins to brown.

Let the enchiladas rest for 5 minutes before you try to scoop them out of the baking dish. I've found that using a spatula on one side and a serving spoon on the other side works very nicely in getting the first one out of the baking dish intact.

Soften the corn tortillas by running a little water over both sides, then stack two or three of them on a plate, cover with a moistened paper towel and steam them in the microwave for 30 to 45 seconds. They'll be soft and pliable, and won't crack when you roll them.

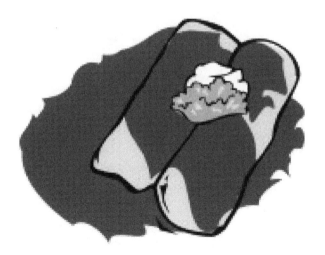

Beef Enchiladas

This is a basic enchilada recipe.

> 1 pound lean ground beef
> 1 small onion, chopped
> 2 Hatch green chiles, roasted, peeled,
>   stemmed, seeded, and chopped
> 1/4 tsp. ground cumin
> 1-1/2 tsp. chili powder
> 2 (10 oz.) cans enchilada sauce, divided
> 1/4 cup vegetable oil
> 10 (6-inch) corn tortillas
> 2 cups shredded Monterey Jack cheese, divided

Preheat the oven to 350 degrees. Lightly spray a 13 x 9 glass baking dish with nonstick cooking spray. Set aside.

Brown the ground beef with the onion and chiles in a 12-inch skillet over medium-high heat. Season with the cumin and chili powder while the meat is cooking.

Place 1/2 cup of the enchilada sauce in a shallow pie pan. Set aside.

Add the oil to a separate 12-inch skillet. Heat for 2 minutes over medium-high heat. Using tongs, fry each tortilla for 3 seconds on each side. Place on paper towels to drain, then stack on a plate.

Dip each tortilla on both sides in the enchilada sauce. Place the dipped tortillas on a separate plate.

Place equal amounts of the beef mixture and 1-1/2 cups of the cheese in the center of each tortilla. Roll up and place seam side down in the prepared baking dish. Pour the remaining enchilada sauce over and sprinkle with the remaining cheese. Cover with aluminum foil and bake for 30 minutes. Remove from the oven and uncover. Return to the oven and bake for 10 more minutes or until the cheese begins to brown.

Saucy Beef Enchiladas

These enchiladas are sauced with a chili gravy.

    1/3 cup all-purpose flour
    1 cup milk
    1-1/2 cups beef broth
    1 pound lean ground beef
    1-1/2 tsp. ground cumin
    1/2 tsp. chili powder
    3 Hatch green chiles, roasted, peeled,
        stemmed, seeded, and chopped
    1/2 cup chopped green onion
    1 cup sour cream
    8 (8-inch) flour tortillas
    1 cup shredded Cheddar cheese, divided

Preheat the oven to 350 degrees. Lightly spray a 13 x 9 glass baking dish with nonstick cooking spray. Set aside.

Whisk the flour and milk together in a small bowl. Pour the mixture into a medium-size saucepan and add the broth. Bring to a boil, stirring. Cook for 5 minutes, then remove the pan from the heat and set aside.

Brown the ground beef in a 12-inch skillet over medium-high heat. Reduce the heat to medium-low. Add half the sauce and the cumin, chili powder, chiles, onion, and sour cream. Heat through.

Warm the tortillas in the microwave for 30 to 45 seconds to make them soft and pliable. Place 1/4 cup of the meat sauce and a generous spoonful of cheese in the center of each tortilla. Roll up and place seam side down in the prepared baking dish.

Pour the remaining sauce and any remaining meat mixture over. Bake for 20 minutes. Remove from the oven and sprinkle with the remaining cheese. Return to the oven and bake for 10 more minutes to melt the cheese.

Enticing Enchiladas

You can easily substitute chicken for the beef in this recipe and use corn tortillas instead of flour tortillas.

2 T. butter
1 small white onion, chopped
3 green onions, chopped
1/2 tsp. garlic powder
1/2 tsp. seasoned salt
4 Hatch green chiles, roasted, peeled,
    stemmed, seeded, and chopped
2 (8 oz.) packages cream cheese, softened
2 cups shredded, cooked beef
8 (8-inch) flour tortillas
2 (10 oz.) cans enchilada sauce
1 (16 oz.) package shredded Monterey Jack cheese

Preheat the oven to 350 degrees. Lightly spray a 13 x 9 glass baking dish with nonstick cooking spray. Set aside.

Melt the butter in a 12-inch skillet over medium heat. Add the white and green onions. Sauté until tender.

Reduce the heat to low. Stir in the garlic powder, seasoned salt, chiles, and cream cheese. Cook, stirring, until the cheese is melted. Stir in the cooked beef. Heat through.

Warm the tortillas in the microwave for 30 to 45 seconds to make them soft and pliable.

Place equal amounts of the beef mixture in the center of each tortilla. Roll up and place seam side down in the prepared baking dish.

Pour the enchilada sauce over, then sprinkle with the cheese. Bake for 35 minutes or until the sauce is bubbly and the cheese begins to brown.

Enchilada Stack

Instead of rolling the tortillas, they are layered.

1/2 pound lean ground beef
1/4 cup finely chopped onion
2 Hatch green chiles, roasted, peeled,
   stemmed, seeded, and chopped
1 (8 oz.) can tomato sauce
1/2 cup water
1-1/2 tsp. chili powder
1/4 tsp. ground cumin
4 (8-inch) flour tortillas
1 cup shredded Cheddar cheese
4 Romaine lettuce leaves
Sour cream

Preheat the oven to 350 degrees. Lightly spray a 1-1/2 quart round casserole dish with nonstick cooking spray. Set aside.

Brown the ground beef with the onion and chiles in a medium-size saucepan over medium-high heat. Stir in the tomato sauce, water, chili powder, and cumin. Bring to a boil, then reduce the heat and simmer for 15 minutes to reduce the sauce, stirring occasionally.

While this is cooking, warm the tortillas in the microwave for 30 to 45 seconds to make them soft and pliable.

Place one of the tortillas in the prepared baking dish. Place one-fourth of the meat mixture and one-fourth of the cheese on the tortilla. Repeat three times. Cover with aluminum foil and bake for 15 minutes. Remove from the oven and uncover. Return to the oven and bake for 10 more minutes to melt the cheese. Cut into quarters and serve on a Romaine lettuce leaf with a dollop of sour cream.

Black Bean 'n' Beef Tortilla Bake

This is a lot like lasagna, made with tortillas.

1 pound lean ground beef
1 small onion, chopped
1 (19 oz.) can enchilada sauce
1 (15 oz.) can black beans, drained and rinsed
1 (8 oz.) can whole kernel corn, drained
2 Hatch green chiles, roasted, peeled,
  stemmed, seeded, and chopped
2 T. chili powder
1 tsp. ground cumin
1 tsp. garlic salt
1/2 tsp. dried oregano
1/4 tsp. black pepper
6 (8-inch) flour tortillas
2 cups shredded Cheddar cheese
1/2 cup chopped cilantro

Brown the ground beef with the onion in a large saucepan over medium heat.

Stir in the enchilada sauce, beans, corn, and chiles. Bring to a boil, then reduce the heat and simmer for 5 minutes.

Stir in the chili powder, cumin, garlic salt, oregano, and pepper. Bring to a boil, then reduce the heat and simmer for 15 minutes, stirring occasionally.

While this is cooking, preheat the oven to 350 degrees. Lightly spray a 13 x 9 glass baking dish with nonstick cooking spray.

Place three tortillas in the prepared baking dish, overlapping as necessary. Place half the meat mixture and half the cheese over the tortillas. Top with the remaining tortillas, meat mixture, and cheese. Bake for 30 minutes or until the cheese begins to brown. Garnish with cilantro.

Pork Enchiladas with Tomatillo Sauce

A green sauce is called a verde sauce and is usually made with tomatillos. Pork goes exceptionally well with a green sauce made with Hatch chiles. It's a marriage made in Hatch Chile Heaven.

1-1/4 pounds pork shoulder, coarsely chopped
10 tomatillos, husked and rinsed
1 T. vegetable oil
1 medium onion, finely chopped
6 Hatch green chiles, roasted, peeled,
   stemmed, seeded, and chopped
2 garlic cloves, crushed
8 (6-inch) corn tortillas, softened
3/4 cup shredded Monterey Jack cheese

Place the pork in a medium-size saucepan and cover with water. Bring to a boil, then reduce the heat and simmer for 40 minutes. Remove the pork to a cutting board, let cool slightly, then shred it with two forks.

While this is cooking, soften the tomatillos in a medium-size saucepan of boiling water for 10 minutes. Drain and set aside.

Preheat the oven to 350 degrees. Lightly spray a 13 x 9 glass baking dish with nonstick cooking spray. Set aside.

Heat the oil in a 12-inch skillet over medium heat. Add the onion and sauté until tender. Add the chiles and garlic. Sauté for one more minute. Add the tomatillos to the onion mixture, stirring constantly, until the tomatillos begin to break up. Reduce the heat and simmer for 10 more minutes. Let cool slightly, then purée in a blender.

Spoon equal amounts of the pork in the center of each tortilla. Roll up and place seam side down in the prepared baking dish. Pour the tomatillo sauce over. Sprinkle with the cheese. Bake for 25 to 30 minutes or until the cheese begins to brown.

Cheesy Chicken Enchiladas

This recipe is easy because of the deli chicken.

1 (19 oz.) can enchilada sauce, divided
3 (1/2-inch thick) slices chicken breast
    (from the deli), cut into one-half inch cubes
3 Hatch green chiles, roasted, peeled,
    stemmed, seeded, and chopped
2 cups shredded Monterey Jack cheese, divided
1 (8 oz.) container sour cream
1 tsp. chili powder
1/4 tsp. cayenne pepper
10 (8-inch) flour tortillas
1/4 cup sliced black olives
1/4 cup chopped green onion

Preheat the oven to 350 degrees. Pour 1/4 cup of the enchilada sauce into a 13 x 9 glass baking dish to cover the bottom. Set aside.

Combine the chicken, chiles, 1-1/2 cups of the cheese, the sour cream, chili powder, and cayenne pepper in a medium-size bowl. Mix well.

Warm the tortillas in the microwave for 30 to 45 seconds to make them soft and pliable. Place 1/4 cup of the chicken mixture in the center of each tortilla. Roll up and place seam side down in the prepared baking dish. Pour the remaining enchilada sauce over and sprinkle with the remaining cheese. Bake for 20 minutes or until the cheese begins to brown.

Top with the olives and green onion.

 Use mesquite turkey (from the deli) instead of chicken for a different flavor.

Colby Chicken Enchiladas

There are no two ways about it and no way around it.
Rolling enchiladas is messy, but the taste is so worth it.

> 2 skinless, boneless chicken breasts,
>   cooked and shredded
> 1-1/2 cups shredded Colby Jack cheese, divided
> 3 Hatch green chiles, roasted, peeled,
>   stemmed, seeded, and chopped
> 1-1/4 cups chopped green onion, divided
> 1 (16 oz.) jar salsa, divided
> 1/4 cup vegetable oil
> 12 (6-inch) corn tortillas

Preheat the oven to 350 degrees. Lightly spray a 13 x 9 glass baking dish with nonstick cooking spray. Set aside.

Combine the chicken, half the cheese, the chiles, and one cup of the onion in a medium-size bowl.

Place half the salsa in a shallow pie pan. Set aside.

Add the oil to a 12-inch skillet. Heat for 2 minutes over medium-high heat. Using tongs, fry each tortilla for 3 seconds on each side. Place on paper towels to drain, then stack on a plate.

Dip each tortilla on both sides in the salsa. Place them on a separate plate.

Place equal amounts of the chicken mixture in the center of each tortilla. Roll up and place them seam side down in the prepared baking dish. Pour the remaining salsa over. Sprinkle with the remaining cheese. Bake for 20 minutes or until the cheese begins to brown.

Garnish with the remaining onion.

Easy Chicken Enchiladas

If you're short on time, but want a dinner that tastes great, this is a quick and easy recipe.

1 (10 oz.) can enchilada sauce, divided
1 (12.5 oz.) can chunk white chicken, drained
1-1/2 cups shredded Cheddar cheese, divided
3 Hatch green chiles, roasted, peeled,
   stemmed, seeded, and chopped
1/4 cup chopped green onion
8 (6-inch) corn tortillas, softened
1/4 cup chopped black olives

Preheat the oven to 350 degrees. Spread 1/4 cup of the enchilada sauce in the bottom of a 13 x 9 glass baking dish. Set aside.

Combine the chicken, one cup of the cheese, the chiles, and onion in a medium-size bowl.

Place equal amounts of the chicken mixture in the center of each tortilla. Roll up and place them seam side down in the prepared baking dish. Pour the remaining sauce over. Sprinkle with the remaining cheese and dot with the olives.

Cover with aluminum foil and bake for 25 to 30 minutes. Remove from the oven and uncover. Return to the oven and bake for 5 more minutes to melt the cheese.

Chicken Enchiladas

This recipe works just as well with pork or beef. You can also substitute corn tortillas instead of flour tortillas.

1 (16 oz.) container sour cream, divided
4 Hatch green chiles, roasted, peeled,
   stemmed, seeded, and chopped
4 green onions, chopped
1/2 cup chopped cilantro
1-1/2 tsp. ground cumin
2 cups diced, cooked chicken
1 (8 oz.) package shredded sharp
   Cheddar cheese, divided
10 (8-inch) flour tortillas, warmed
1 (8 oz.) package cream cheese, cut
   lengthwise into 10 strips
1 (19 oz.) can enchilada sauce

Preheat the oven to 350 degrees. Lightly spray a 13 x 9 glass baking dish with nonstick cooking spray. Set aside.

Combine 1-3/4 cups of the sour cream, the chiles, onions, cilantro, cumin, chicken, and 1/2 cup of the Cheddar cheese in a large bowl.

Place equal amounts of the mixture in the center of each tortilla. Add a cream cheese strip. Roll up and place seam side down in the prepared baking dish.

Pour the enchilada sauce over. Cover with aluminum foil and bake for 30 minutes. Remove from the oven and uncover. Sprinkle the remaining cheese on top. Return to the oven and bake for 10 minutes or until the cheese begins to brown.

Top with a dollop of the remaining sour cream.

Creamy Chicken Enchiladas

Chicken, chiles, cheese, onions, beans, spices, and seasonings all combine to create a delicious recipe.

2 skinless, boneless chicken breasts
1 chicken bouillon cube
2 bay leaves
1/4 tsp. black pepper
1/4 tsp. chili powder
1/4 tsp. dried oregano
2 T. butter
1 cup chopped onion
1 garlic clove, minced
4 Hatch green chiles, roasted, peeled,
    stemmed, seeded, and chopped
1 (15 oz.) can black beans, drained and rinsed
1 tsp. ground cumin
1 (8 oz.) package cream cheese, cut into chunks
8 (8-inch) flour tortillas, warmed
1 (10 oz.) can enchilada sauce
1 cup shredded Cheddar cheese

Place the chicken in a medium-size saucepan and cover with water. Add the bouillon cube, bay leaves, pepper, chili powder, and oregano. Bring to a boil, then reduce the heat and simmer for 15 minutes or until the chicken is cooked through. Discard the bay leaves. Remove the chicken to a cutting board, let cool, then shred it with two forks. Set aside.

Preheat the oven to 350 degrees. Lightly spray a 13 x 9 glass baking dish with nonstick cooking spray. Set aside.

Melt the butter in a 12-inch skillet over medium heat. Add the onion and sauté until tender. Add the garlic and chiles. Sauté for one more minute. Stir in the beans, chicken, cumin, and cream cheese. Heat through, but do not boil.

Place equal amounts of the mixture in the center of each tortilla. Roll up and place seam side down in the prepared baking dish. Pour the enchilada sauce over and sprinkle with the cheese. Cover with aluminum foil and bake for 30 minutes. Remove from the oven and uncover. Return to the oven and bake for 10 more minutes to melt the cheese.

 Don't toss the chicken broth used for poaching the chicken. There's a lot of flavor there. Reserve it for another use in a recipe that calls for chicken broth.

Easy Enchiladas

Just roll, bake, and serve.

1 (12.5 oz.) can chunk white chicken, drained
2 Hatch green chiles, roasted, peeled,
   stemmed, seeded, and chopped
1 (10 oz.) can green enchilada sauce, divided
10 (6-inch) corn tortillas, softened
1 cup shredded Monterey Jack cheese

Preheat the oven to 350 degrees. Lightly spray a 13 x 9 glass baking dish with nonstick cooking spray. Set aside.

Combine the chicken, chiles, and 1/4 cup of the enchilada sauce in a medium-size bowl. Place equal amounts of the mixture in the center of each tortilla. Roll up and place seam side down in the prepared baking dish.

Pour the remaining enchilada sauce over. Sprinkle with cheese. Bake for 25 minutes or until heated through and the cheese begins to brown.

Shrimp Enchiladas

Shrimp and sliced mushrooms make these enchiladas very different and delicious.

2 cups chicken broth
12 large shrimp, peeled, deveined,
   and cut into bite-size pieces
2 T. butter
1 small onion, chopped
1 (8 oz.) container sliced mushrooms,
   coarsely chopped
1 garlic clove, minced
2 T. all-purpose flour
1/2 tsp. salt
1/4 tsp. black pepper
1 cup **Green Chile Sauce** (page 287)
4 Hatch green chiles, roasted, peeled,
   stemmed, seeded, and chopped
12 (6-inch) corn tortillas
1 (8 oz.) package shredded Monterey
   Jack cheese
1 small tomato, chopped
2 green onions, sliced
1 lime, cut into wedges

Preheat the oven to 350 degrees. Lightly spray a 13 x 9 glass baking dish with nonstick cooking spray. Set aside.

Pour the broth into a medium-size saucepan. Bring to a simmer and add the shrimp. Cook for 3 to 4 minutes or until pink. Remove the shrimp to a bowl and reserve the broth in a separate bowl.

Melt the butter in a 12-inch skillet over medium heat. Add the onion and mushrooms. Sauté until tender.

Add the garlic and sauté for one more minute.

Stir in the flour. Add one cup of the reserved chicken broth. Bring to a boil, stirring constantly to incorporate the flour, then reduce the heat and simmer until thickened.

Stir in the shrimp, salt, and pepper. Remove the pan from the heat and set aside.

Place the Green Chile Sauce, chiles, and one cup of the remaining broth in a blender or a food processor. Blend until smooth. Place the mixture in a small saucepan and keep warm.

Soften the tortillas by steaming them in the microwave.

Dip the tortillas, one at a time, in the chile mixture. Place equal amounts of the shrimp mixture in the center of each tortilla. Roll up and place seam side down in the prepared baking dish.

Pour the remaining sauce over and sprinkle with the cheese. Bake for 25 minutes.

Garnish with the chopped tomatoes and green onions. Place a lime wedge on the side.

Juicing the enchiladas with a squirt of lime juice adds a nice zing and fresh taste.

Snappy Seafood Enchiladas

This recipe comes together in a snap.

2 T. butter
4 green onions, chopped
1 red bell pepper, chopped
2 Hatch green chiles, roasted, peeled,
  stemmed, seeded, and chopped
1 garlic clove, minced
4 medium tomatoes, chopped
1 pound red snapper, flaked
Salt and freshly ground black pepper
10 (6-inch) corn tortillas, softened
1 (8 oz.) package shredded Monterey
  Jack cheese, divided
1 (16 oz.) jar tomatillo sauce or
  Hatch green enchilada sauce
Sour cream
1 lime, cut into wedges

Preheat the oven to 350 degrees. Lightly spray a 13 x 9 glass baking dish with nonstick cooking spray. Set aside.

Melt the butter in a 12-inch skillet over medium-high heat. Add the onions and bell pepper. Sauté for 3 minutes. Stir in the chiles, garlic, and tomatoes. Cook for one more minute. Add the snapper and cook for 5 minutes. Season with salt and pepper to taste.

Place equal amounts of the mixture in the center of each tortilla. Sprinkle some cheese over the mixture. Roll up and place seam side down in the prepared baking dish.

Pour the tomatillo sauce over. Sprinkle with the remaining cheese. Bake for 10 to 15 minutes or until heated through.

Serve with sour cream and a lime wedge.

Beef and Pork

Bistec Ranchero

Bistec Ranchero is steak cooked with tomatoes, onions, and chiles to make a flavorful sauce. It's sometimes simmered in water, then cut into strips; other times it's cut into strips before cooking. Either way you slice it, this Bistec Ranchero is delicious.

1 T. vegetable oil
3 medium tomatoes, sliced
1 medium onion, thinly sliced
4 Hatch green chiles, roasted, peeled,
   stemmed, seeded, and chopped
4 sirloin steaks, thinly sliced
Salt and freshly ground black pepper

Heat the oil in a 12-inch skillet over medium heat. Add the tomatoes, onion, and chiles. Cook for 3 to 4 minutes.

Add the meat and stir well to mix with the vegetables. Cook for 8 minutes or until the meat is almost cooked. Reduce the heat to medium-low and simmer for 5 more minutes. Season with salt and pepper to taste.

Perfect Pot Roast

This hearty, nourishing pot roast, flavored with Hatch chiles, is perfect on a cold night.

2 pounds rump roast
1-3/4 tsp. salt
3 garlic cloves, pressed
1/4 tsp. dried oregano
1/2 tsp. chili powder
1/8 tsp. black pepper
1 T. olive oil
2 T. vegetable oil
1 tomato, coarsely chopped
1 onion, coarsely chopped
4 Hatch green chiles, roasted, peeled,
   stemmed, seeded, and chopped
10 black olives, pitted and chopped
2 tsp. capers
1/3 cup tomato sauce
2-1/2 cups beef broth
3 carrots, thickly sliced
6 medium red potatoes, peeled
   and quartered

Rub the meat with the salt, then with the garlic, oregano, chili powder, pepper, and olive oil. Place the meat in a bowl and cover with plastic wrap. Marinate in the refrigerator for 30 minutes to 2 hours, turning occasionally.

Heat the vegetable oil in a Dutch oven over medium-high heat. Brown the meat on all sides, then remove and set aside.

Reduce the heat to medium-low. Add the tomato, onion, and chiles. Cook for 5 minutes. Add the olives, capers, and tomato sauce. Cook for 5 more minutes.

Return the meat to the pan, along with any accumulated juices. Add the broth and bring to a boil. Reduce the heat, cover, and simmer for 1-1/2 hours, stirring and turning the meat occasionally.

Add the carrots and potatoes. Simmer for 30 to 40 more minutes or until the potatoes and carrots are tender and the sauce has thickened.

Serve on a platter with the vegetables on the side.

Green Chile Goulash

A perfect weeknight supper.

  1 pound lean ground beef
  1 medium onion, chopped
  3 Hatch green chiles, roasted, peeled,
     stemmed, seeded, and chopped
  1/4 tsp. ground cumin
  1 T. chili powder
  1 (8 oz.) can tomato sauce
  1 (14.5 oz.) can stewed tomatoes
  3 cups cooked elbow macaroni
  1 cup shredded Cheddar cheese

Brown the ground beef with the onion and chiles in a 12-inch skillet over medium-high heat. Season with the cumin and chili powder while the meat is cooking.

Stir in the tomato sauce and tomatoes. Bring to a boil, then reduce the heat and simmer for 10 minutes, stirring occasionally.

Add the cooked macaroni and heat through. Sprinkle with cheese.

Green Chile Meatballs

This is the Hatch version of spaghetti and meatballs.

1 pound lean ground beef
1/2 cup bread crumbs
2 T. finely chopped cilantro
1/2 cup minced onion
Pinch of salt and pepper
2 T. olive oil
3 cups water, divided
3 T. chopped chives
1/2 cup finely sliced green onion
2 garlic cloves, minced
2 tsp. beef bouillon
1 (14.5 oz.) can diced tomatoes
2 Hatch green chiles, roasted, peeled,
    stemmed, seeded, and chopped
2 cups cooked white rice, hot

Combine the ground beef, bread crumbs, cilantro, minced onion, salt, and pepper in a medium-size bowl. Shape into small meatballs.

Heat the oil in a 12-inch skillet over medium-high heat. Add the meatballs and brown on all sides.

Reduce the heat to low, add 1/2 of the cup water, cover, and steam for 10 minutes. Remove the meatballs to a plate and set aside.

Add the remaining water to the skillet, stirring to scrape up the flavorful brown bits from the bottom of the skillet.

Add the chives, green onion, garlic, bouillon, and tomatoes. Bring to a boil, then reduce the heat and simmer for 10 minutes, stirring occasionally.

Return the meatballs to the skillet, along with any accumulated juices. Add the chiles. Simmer for 30 minutes, stirring occasionally. Serve over rice.

 *For a variation, make **Hatch Meatballs,** a.k.a. Albondigas. Chop 4 slices bacon into small pieces. Add to one pound lean ground beef. Mix in one beaten egg, 1/4 cup minced onion, 1/4 cup bread crumbs, and 2 roasted Hatch green chiles, peeled, seeded, and chopped. Shape into balls and place in a pan of boiling water or beef broth and boil until cooked. Remove with a slotted spoon.*

Quickie Casserole

A few ingredients, a few minutes, and dinner is on the table.

> 1 pound lean ground beef
> 1 small onion, chopped
> 1 T. chili powder
> 1 garlic clove, minced
> 3 Hatch green chiles, roasted, peeled,
>   stemmed, seeded, and chopped
> 1 (14.5 oz.) can diced tomatoes
> 2 cups cooked white rice, hot
> 1 cup slightly crushed corn chips
> 1 (8 oz.) package shredded Colby Jack cheese

Brown the ground beef with the onion in a 12-inch skillet over medium-high heat. Season with the chili powder while the meat is cooking. Add the garlic and chiles. Cook for one more minute.

Stir in the tomatoes. Bring to a boil, then reduce the heat and simmer for 5 minutes. Serve over cooked rice. Top with the corn chips and cheese.

Stuffed Bell Peppers

Topped with Monterey Jack cheese, these stuffed peppers make a delicious dinner served with rice and beans.

4 green or red bell peppers, stemmed and seeded
1 pound lean ground beef
2 Hatch green chiles, roasted, peeled,
   stemmed, seeded, and chopped
3/4 cup shredded Monterey Jack cheese, divided
1 (2.25 oz.) can chopped black olives, drained
1/2 cup bread crumbs

Preheat the oven to 350 degrees. Lightly spray a 13 x 9 glass baking dish with nonstick cooking spray. Set aside.

Soften the bell peppers by parboiling or steaming them for 10 to 15 minutes.

Combine the ground beef, chiles, 1/2 cup of the cheese, olives, and bread crumbs in a medium-size bowl.

Place equal amounts of the mixture into the bell peppers. Top with the remaining cheese. Bake for 45 minutes.

 You can substitute ground turkey or shredded chicken for the ground beef.

Chile Rellenos Casserole

Instead of trying to stuff Hatch chiles (which can be next to impossible), they are split open and layered in a casserole, along with ground beef, corn, and black beans.

1 pound lean ground beef
1 medium onion, chopped
1 garlic clove, minced
1 cup frozen corn, thawed
1 T. ground cumin
1 T. chili powder
1 (15 oz.) can black beans, drained and rinsed
1-3/4 cups salsa
2 Hatch green chiles, roasted, peeled,
    stemmed, seeded, and chopped
8 Hatch green chiles, roasted, peeled,
    stemmed, seeded, and split open
1 cup shredded Monterey Jack cheese
Sour cream

Preheat the oven to 350 degrees. Lightly spray an 8 x 8 glass baking dish with nonstick cooking spray. Set aside.

Brown the ground beef with the onion in a 12-inch skillet over medium-high heat.

Add the garlic, corn, cumin, and chili powder. Cook for one more minute.

Stir in the beans, salsa, and two chopped chiles. Bring to a boil and cook, stirring, for 3 minutes.

Lay four of the split chiles in the bottom of the prepared baking dish. Add half the meat filling and half the cheese. Repeat. Bake for 15 minutes or until the cheese begins to brown.

Serve with a dollop or two of sour cream.

Refried Tortilla Chip Casserole

This casserole comes together quickly and has the flavor of baked nachos. Tortilla chips and refried beans are mixed in with the beef and sauce.

1 pound lean ground beef
1 cup chopped onion
2 Hatch green chiles, roasted, peeled,
  stemmed, seeded, and chopped
2 T. chili powder
1 T. ground cumin
1 (14.5 oz.) can diced tomatoes
1 (16 oz.) can refried beans
1 (10 oz.) bag tortilla chips, crushed
1 cup shredded Cheddar cheese
1 cup shredded Monterey Jack cheese

Preheat the oven to 350 degrees. Lightly spray a 13 x 9 glass baking dish with nonstick cooking spray. Set aside.

Brown the ground beef with the onion and chiles in a 12-inch skillet over high heat. Season with chili powder and cumin while the meat is cooking. Stir in the tomatoes. Bring to a boil, then reduce the heat and simmer for 5 minutes, stirring occasionally.

Spread the beans evenly in the prepared baking dish. Sprinkle with half the tortilla chips. Top with the beef mixture, then sprinkle with the remaining chips and top with the Cheddar and Monterey Jack cheeses. Bake for 25 minutes or until the cheese is lightly brown. Let rest for 5 minutes before serving.

 Top with chopped tomatoes, chopped green onion, avocado slices, and sour cream.

South of the Border Casserole

This casserole features a creamy cheese filling made with ricotta cheese and sour cream, similar to the filling used in a lasagna.

1-1/2 cups crushed Nachos chips
1-1/2 pounds lean ground beef
1 medium onion, chopped
1 garlic clove, chopped
1 (10 oz.) can enchilada sauce
1 cup sour cream
1 cup ricotta cheese
1 medium egg, beaten
1/4 cup chopped cilantro
3 Hatch green chiles, roasted, peeled,
   stemmed, seeded, and chopped
1 cup shredded Monterey Jack cheese
1 cup shredded Cheddar cheese
1/4 cup sliced black olives

Preheat the oven to 350 degrees. Lightly spray a 13 x 9 glass baking dish with nonstick cooking spray. Sprinkle the Nachos over the bottom of the prepared baking dish. Set aside.

Brown the ground beef in a 12-inch skillet over medium-high heat. Add the onion and garlic halfway through cooking.

Stir in the enchilada sauce. Heat through.

Combine the sour cream, ricotta cheese, egg, cilantro, and chiles in a medium-size bowl.

Place half the ground beef mixture over the Nachos in the prepared baking dish. Spread the sour cream mixture over and top with the remaining meat mixture. Cover with the Monterey Jack and Cheddar cheeses. Dot with olives. Bake for 40 to 45 minutes.

Salsa Beef Stew

This beef stew is a hearty meal with a nice kick that will warm you on the inside. If you want an even bigger kick, add more chiles.

2 T. olive oil
2 pounds stew beef cubes
1 large onion, coarsely chopped
4 Hatch green chiles, roasted, peeled, stemmed, seeded, and chopped
1 garlic clove, minced
2 cups beef broth
1 (14.5 oz.) can diced tomatoes
1/2 cup chunky salsa
3 T. cornstarch
1/4 cup cold water
Salt and freshly ground black pepper
3 cups cooked white rice, hot
2 green onions, sliced

Heat the oil in a Dutch oven over medium-high heat. Add the beef and brown it on all sides. Remove and set aside.

Add the onion to the pan. Sauté until the onion is tender. Add the chiles and garlic. Sauté for one more minute.

Return the beef to the pan, along with any accumulated juices. Stir in the broth, tomatoes, and salsa. Bring to a boil, then reduce the heat, cover, and simmer for 2-1/2 hours, stirring occasionally.

Mix the cornstarch with the cold water in a small bowl until it forms a smooth paste. Stir the mixture slowly into the stew. Bring the heat up to medium-high, stirring until thickened. Season with salt and pepper to taste.

Serve over rice. Garnish with the onions.

Stuffed Poblano Peppers

Chile Rellenos are poblano peppers stuffed with cheese. Hatch chiles are included in the stuffing.

1 (8 oz.) can tomato sauce
1 (14.5 oz.) can diced tomatoes
2 T. chili powder
1 pound lean ground beef
1 (15 oz.) can black beans, drained,
  rinsed, and slightly mashed
1/2 cup instant rice, cooked
1/4 cup chopped onion
2 Hatch green chiles, roasted, peeled,
  stemmed, seeded, and chopped
2 large poblano peppers, stemmed,
  seeded, and sliced in half
1/2 cup shredded Cheddar cheese

Preheat the oven to 350 degrees. Lightly spray a 13 x 9 glass baking dish with nonstick cooking spray. Set aside.

Combine the tomato sauce, tomatoes, and chili powder in a medium-size bowl. Remove and reserve 1/4 cup of this mixture.

Combine the ground beef, beans, rice, onion, and chiles in a large bowl.

Combine the tomato mixture with the beef mixture. Stuff each half of the poblano peppers with the meat-tomato mixture. Place the peppers in the prepared baking dish and top with the reserved tomato mixture. Bake for one hour.

Remove from the oven and sprinkle the cheese on top of the peppers. Return to the oven and bake for 5 more minutes or until the cheese melts.

Salsa Style Meatloaf

This is not your average Monday night meatloaf. The crushed tortilla chips add a nice flavor and texture—much better than bread crumbs. You can also use this recipe to make mini meatloaves… just shape the meat into balls and bake in a muffin tin.

2 pounds lean ground beef
1 large egg, lightly beaten
2 cups crushed tortilla chips
4 Hatch green chiles, roasted, peeled,
   stemmed, seeded, and chopped
1-1/2 cups salsa, divided
1/2 cup shredded Cheddar cheese
2 T. chopped cilantro

Preheat the oven to 350 degrees. Lightly spray a 9-inch loaf pan with nonstick cooking spray. Set aside.

Combine the ground beef, egg, tortilla chips, chiles, half the salsa, the cheese, and cilantro in a large bowl.

Place in the prepared baking pan and shape into a loaf. Cover with the remaining salsa. Bake for one hour. Let rest for 10 minutes before slicing.

Place 2 onions, quartered, and two green bell peppers, stemmed, seeded, and quartered, around the sides of the baking dish.

Dijon Bacon Meatloaf

Bacon tops this delicious meatloaf seasoned with chiles and Dijon mustard.

2-1/2 pounds lean ground beef
1 medium onion, diced
5 garlic cloves, minced
8 Hatch green chiles, roasted, peeled,
   stemmed, seeded, and chopped
1/4 cup Dijon mustard
1/2 cup ketchup, divided
2 T. fresh thyme leaves
2 medium eggs, lightly beaten
2 cups bread crumbs
Salt and freshly ground black pepper
6 slices bacon

Preheat the oven to 350 degrees. Lightly spray a 9-inch loaf pan with nonstick cooking spray. Set aside.

Combine the ground beef, onion, garlic, chiles, mustard, 1/4 cup of the ketchup, the thyme, eggs, and bread crumbs in a large bowl. Season with salt and pepper to taste.

Place in the prepared baking pan. Shape into a loaf. Cover with the remaining ketchup and place the bacon slices on top. Bake for one hour. Let rest for 10 minutes before slicing.

Barbecue Style Meatloaf

*If you like barbecued burgers, you'll love this meatloaf.
Serve with mashed potatoes and a veggie, such as carrots
or green beans.*

2 pounds lean ground beef
1 medium onion, finely minced
1 green bell pepper, finely minced
1 (14.5 oz.) can diced tomatoes, divided
4 Hatch green chiles, roasted, peeled,
    stemmed, seeded, and chopped
1 large egg, lightly beaten
1 cup bread crumbs
1 tsp. salt
1 tsp. black pepper
1 tsp. ground cumin
1 tsp. chili powder
1 tsp. cayenne pepper
1/2 cup barbecue sauce

Preheat the oven to 350 degrees. Lightly spray a 9-inch loaf
pan with nonstick cooking spray. Set aside.

Combine the ground beef, onion, bell pepper, 1/2 cup of the
tomatoes, the chiles, egg, bread crumbs, salt, pepper, cumin, chili
powder, cayenne pepper, and barbecue sauce in a large bowl.

Place in the prepared baking pan. Shape into a loaf. Cover
with the remaining tomatoes. Bake for one hour and 15 minutes.
Let rest for 10 minutes before slicing.

*You can get really creative with this recipe. Use
a red bell pepper instead of the green bell pepper.
Add shredded carrots and/or zucchini for moistness
and sweetness. To make* **Salsa Meatloaf,** *use salsa
instead of barbecue sauce.*

Beef 'n' Black Beans

Served on a bed of rice and topped with cheese, this recipe is simple to make and super delicious.

1 pound lean ground beef
1 medium onion, chopped
1 T. chili powder
1/2 tsp. garlic salt
1 (14.5 oz.) can diced tomatoes
1 (8 oz.) can whole kernel corn, drained
1 (15 oz.) can black beans, drained and rinsed
2 Hatch green chiles, roasted, peeled,
    stemmed, seeded, and chopped
1-1/2 cups cooked white rice, hot
1 cup shredded Cheddar cheese

Brown the ground beef with the onion in a 12-inch skillet over medium-high heat. Season with the chili powder and garlic salt while the meat is cooking.

Stir in the tomatoes, corn, beans, and chiles. Bring to a boil, then reduce the heat and simmer for 10 minutes, stirring occasionally.

Serve over rice. Sprinkle the cheese over the top.

Santa Fe Beef Stroganoff

The addition of Hatch chiles can transform any recipe.

1 cup all-purpose flour
1/4 tsp. garlic powder
1/2 T. black pepper
2 pounds round steak, cut into cubes
4 T. butter, divided
1 medium onion, chopped
1 (8 oz.) container sliced mushrooms
2 cups beef broth
4 Hatch green chiles, roasted, peeled,
    stemmed, seeded, and chopped
1 cup sour cream
1 (8 oz.) package egg noodles, cooked, hot
2 T. chopped cilantro

Mix the flour, garlic powder, and black pepper on a dinner plate. Dredge the meat in the flour mixture.

Melt 3 T. of the butter in a 12-inch skillet over medium-high heat. Add the beef, in batches, and brown it on all sides. Remove and set aside.

Melt the remaining butter in the skillet. Add the onion and mushrooms. Sauté until the onion is tender and the mushrooms are browned.

Stir in the broth. Return the meat to the skillet, along with any accumulated juices. Bring to a boil, then reduce the heat, cover, and simmer for 2 hours, stirring occasionally.

Stir in the chiles. Simmer for 10 more minutes, uncovered. Remove the pan from the heat and stir in the sour cream.

Serve over noodles. Garnish with cilantro.

Beef and Beans

This recipe has it all... meat, veggies, chiles, rice, and beans, topped with crunchy corn chips.

    2 T. olive oil
    1-1/2 pounds stew beef cubes
    1 medium onion, chopped
    1 garlic clove, minced
    1 (14.5 oz.) can diced tomatoes
    4 Hatch green chiles, roasted, peeled,
        stemmed, seeded, and chopped
    1 (15.5 oz.) can dark red kidney
        beans, drained and rinsed
    1 cup frozen corn, thawed
    1/2 cup sliced black olives
    1/2 cup water
    2 T. chili powder
    1/2 tsp. salt
    1/4 tsp. black pepper
    1 cup shredded Cheddar cheese
    3 cups cooked white rice, hot
    1 cup crushed corn chips

Heat the oil in a 12-inch skillet over medium-high heat. Add the beef and brown it on all sides.

Add the onion. Sauté until tender. Add the garlic and sauté for one more minute.

Stir in the tomatoes, chiles, beans, corn, olives, water, chili powder, salt, and pepper. Bring to a boil, then reduce the heat, cover, and simmer for 45 minutes, stirring occasionally.

Top with cheese. Cover and let cook for 3 minutes or until the cheese melts. Serve over rice. Sprinkle with the chips.

Swiss Steak

This is so tender that it just melts in your mouth.

1/4 cup all-purpose flour
1/4 tsp. salt
1 tsp. black pepper
1-1/2 pounds bottom round steak, tenderized
2 T. vegetable oil
1 medium onion, chopped
2 carrots, finely chopped
1/2 red bell pepper, finely chopped
2 garlic cloves, minced
1 (14.5 oz.) can beef broth
2 (14.5 oz.) cans diced tomatoes
4 Hatch green chiles, roasted, peeled,
   stemmed, seeded, and chopped
1 T. Worcestershire sauce (optional)

Mix the flour with the salt and pepper on a dinner plate. Dredge the meat in the flour mixture.

Heat the oil in a 12-inch skillet over medium heat. Add the meat and brown it on both sides. Remove to a plate and set aside.

Add the onion, carrots, and bell pepper to the skillet. Sauté until the vegetables are tender-crisp, adding more oil if necessary. Add the garlic and sauté for one more minute.

Add the broth and stir to deglaze the skillet. Return the meat to the skillet. Add the tomatoes, chiles, and Worcestershire sauce, if using. Bring to a boil, then reduce the heat, cover, and simmer for 45 minutes, stirring occasionally, or until the meat is tender.

Tenderize the steak by beating the heck out of it with a meat mallet.

Salisbury Steak

This is basic comfort food. Serve with mashed potatoes and a vegetable.

1-1/2 pounds lean ground beef
1 small onion, chopped
3 Hatch green chiles, roasted, peeled,
    stemmed, seeded, and chopped
1 large egg, lightly beaten
1/2 cup bread crumbs
1/4 cup salsa
2 T. taco seasoning
2 T. chopped cilantro, divided
1 (2.75 oz.) package country-style gravy mix
1-1/2 cups beef broth or water
1 (14.5 oz.) can diced tomatoes

Combine the ground beef, onion, chiles, egg, bread crumbs, salsa, taco seasoning, and half the cilantro in a large bowl. Shape the mixture into six patties.

Heat a 12-inch nonstick skillet over medium-high heat. When the skillet is hot, add the patties, in batches, and brown them on both sides. Remove to a plate and set aside.

Whisk the gravy mix, broth, tomatoes, and the remaining cilantro together in a medium-size bowl. Pour into the skillet and cook for 5 minutes, stirring occasionally, or until thickened. Return the meat to the skillet, scooping the gravy mixture over the patties. Cook for 10 more minutes, turning once or twice.

You can substitute a brown gravy mix instead of the country gravy mix. For a smoother gravy, purée the diced tomatoes.

Chipotle Brisket

Cooked in a crock pot, this is an easy meal to prepare.

1 (6-pound) brisket, trimmed of visible
  fat and cut into two-inch pieces
1-1/2 T. chipotle powder
1 T. ground cumin
Salt and freshly ground black pepper
8 Hatch green chiles, roasted, peeled,
  stemmed, seeded, and chopped
1 large onion, chopped
4 garlic cloves, minced
2/3 cup finely chopped cilantro
Juice of one lime

Place the brisket in a crock pot. Sprinkle with the chipotle powder, cumin, and the salt and pepper to taste. Rub the spice mixture into meat. Add the chiles, onion, garlic, and cilantro. Sprinkle with lime juice and mix all the ingredients together. Cover and cook on high for 8 hours.

This also works very well as a filling for **Shredded Brisket Tacos.** *Shred the meat and fill warmed flour tortillas with a mixture of brisket and lightly sautéed onions and corn. Sprinkle with chopped cilantro and squeeze some fresh lime juice over.*

Tender Tex-Mex Pork

The pork will be very tender. If you have leftovers, which you probably won't because it's so good, shred the pork and use it in a bean and cheese quesadilla or wrap it in a soft flour tortilla with chopped lettuce, tomatoes, and cheese.

4 T. olive oil
4 T. chili powder
4 T. crushed red pepper flakes
1 T. dried oregano
1 tsp. seasoned salt
1 tsp. ground cumin
2 garlic cloves, crushed
4 T. chopped cilantro
1 T. black pepper
1/2 cup chopped red onion
1/2 cup chopped green onion
1 (4 pound) pork loin, cut
  into two-inch cubes
1 (14 oz.) can chicken broth
2 Hatch green chiles, roasted, peeled,
  stemmed, seeded, and chopped

Combine the oil, chili powder, red pepper flakes, oregano, seasoned salt, cumin, garlic, cilantro, pepper, and the red and green onion in a large bowl.

Add the pork and coat it evenly with the marinade. Cover with plastic wrap and marinate in the refrigerator for 4 hours, stirring once or twice to evenly coat the pork.

Preheat the oven to 350 degrees.

Place the pork in a roasting pan. Add the broth and chiles. Cover with aluminum foil. Bake for 3-1/2 to 4 hours, stirring once halfway through cooking.

Pinto Pork

This recipe takes all day to cook. Start it early in the morning.

2 (16 oz.) packages dried pinto
  beans, rinsed
1 (2 pound) boneless pork roast
4 T. chili powder
3 T. ground cumin
2 tsp. dried oregano
1/2 cup picante sauce
4 Hatch green chiles, roasted, peeled,
  stemmed, seeded, and chopped
2 garlic cloves, minced
Salt and freshly ground black pepper
2 cups corn chips
3 green onions, sliced
1 large tomato, diced
1 cup shredded Cheddar cheese
1 avocado, peeled, pitted, and coarsely chopped

Preheat the oven to 275 degrees.

Place the beans, pork, chili powder, cumin, oregano, picante sauce, chiles, and garlic in a large roasting pan. Cover with water. Bake for 10 to 12 hours, stirring every hour and turning the roast.

Remove the meat to a cutting board and shred it with two forks. Return it to the bean mixture. Season with salt and pepper to taste. Stir to mix. Return to the oven and heat through.

Serve over corn chips. Top with the onions, tomato, cheese, and avocado.

If you don't want to heat up your house all day, cook this in a crock pot. Brown the meat first.

Green Chile Stew with Green Apples and Sage

This recipe comes from my friend, Dee. Serve this delicious stew with a side of cornbread.

2 T. olive oil
2-1/2 pound pork loin, trimmed
   and cut into one-inch cubes
1 medium onion, diced
1 red bell pepper, chopped
4 garlic cloves, minced
2 cups water
3 green Granny Smith apples,
   cored, seeded, and chopped
8 Hatch green chiles, roasted, peeled,
   stemmed, seeded, and chopped
5 fresh sage leaves, cut into slices
1 tsp. salt
1/2 tsp. celery salt
Queso Cojita cheese, grated

Heat the oil in a Dutch oven over medium heat. Add the pork and brown it on all sides. Add the onion, bell pepper, and garlic. Sauté until the onion and bell pepper are tender.

Add the water, apples, chiles, sage, salt, and celery salt. Stir to mix. Bring to a boil, then reduce the heat, cover, and simmer for 30 minutes, stirring occasionally. Uncover and simmer for 30 more minutes, stirring occasionally, or until the pork is tender. Add water as needed. This stew should be thick. Garnish with the cheese.

Queso Cojita is a semi-soft Mexican white cheese. Substitute Asadero or Monterey Jack cheese.

Tomatillo Pork

Started on the stove, then cooked in a crock pot, this savory stew is flavored with tomatillos. Add more or less Hatch chiles to vary the heat level.

1/3 cup all-purpose flour
1 tsp. ground cumin
1 tsp. salt
1/4 tsp. black pepper
1 tsp. ground sage
2-1/2 pounds pork stew meat,
    cut into one-inch cubes
2 T. vegetable oil
3 T. vinegar
2 cups coarsely chopped onions
3 cups peeled and diced potatoes
2 cups coarsely chopped tomatillos
8 Hatch green chiles, roasted, peeled,
    stemmed, seeded, and chopped
1 (14 oz.) can chicken broth
1 tsp. brown sugar

Mix the flour, cumin, salt, pepper, and sage in a plastic Zip-lock bag. Add the pork, seal the bag, and shake to coat the pork.

Heat the oil in a 12-inch skillet over medium-high heat. Add the pork in batches and brown on all sides. Remove and set aside.

Add the vinegar to the skillet, stirring and scraping up the brown bits.

Place the onions, potatoes, tomatillos, chiles, broth, brown sugar, pork, and the vinegar mixture from the skillet, into a crock pot. Stir to mix, then cover and cook on low for 8 to 10 hours or on high for 4 to 5 hours.

Easy Cheesy Pork Chops

Just a few simple ingredients come together for a tender, delicious, and juicy pork chop flavored with garlic and chiles, and topped with melted cheese. Serve with rice and a side of beans.

4 thick-cut pork chops
2 garlic cloves, minced
Salt and freshly ground black pepper
2 Hatch green chiles, roasted, peeled,
    stemmed, seeded, and cut in half
1/2 cup shredded Longhorn cheese
1/2 cup shredded Monterey Jack cheese

Preheat the oven to 375 degrees.

Place the pork in a 13 x 9 glass baking dish. Using a sharp knife, cut four to five slits in each pork chop. Place the minced garlic into the slits. Season with salt and pepper to taste.

Bake for 45 minutes or until the meat is cooked through.

Remove from the oven and place one-half of a green chile slice on each pork chop. Sprinkle the Longhorn and Monterey Jack cheeses evenly over the pork chops. Return to the oven for 5 minutes to melt the cheese.

To make this meal even easier, put the garlic-stuffed pork chops in a crock pot and cook on low for 8 hours. If you've never had pork chops cooked in a slow cooker by themselves, you are in for a real taste treat. Add the green chile and cheese. Cook for 10 to 15 more minutes to warm the chile and melt the cheese.

Mexican Pork Chops

This is one of my favorite recipes. I serve it over rice with a side of pinto beans and a few dollops of sour cream.

> 2 T. olive oil
> 1 tsp. fajita seasoning, divided
> 1 tsp. black pepper, divided
> 2 T. chili powder, divided
> 1 tsp. ground cumin, divided
> 4 center loin pork chops, trimmed of fat
> 1 medium onion, chopped
> 3 Hatch green chiles, roasted, peeled,
>   stemmed, seeded, and chopped
> 1 garlic clove, minced
> 1-1/2 cups water
> 1 (14.5 oz.) can Mexican style diced tomatoes
> 2 cups cooked white rice, hot
> 1 cup shredded Cheddar cheese
> 1/2 cup sour cream

Heat the oil in a 12-inch skillet over medium-high heat. Sprinkle half the fajita seasoning, pepper, chili powder, and cumin over both sides of the pork chops. Place them in the skillet and brown them on both sides. Remove and set aside.

Add the onion, chiles, and garlic to the skillet. Season with the remaining fajita seasoning, pepper, chili powder, and cumin. Sauté in the pork drippings until tender.

Stir in the water and tomatoes. Bring to a boil, then reduce the heat, cover, and simmer for 5 minutes to blend the flavors.

Return the pork chops, along with any accumulated juices, to the skillet, spooning the sauce over. Bring to a boil, then reduce the heat and simmer for 30 minutes or until the pork is tender, stirring occasionally.

Serve over rice and sprinkle with the cheese. Top with a dollop of sour cream.

 *To make **Mexican Chicken Chops**, use 4 skinless, boneless chicken breasts instead of the pork chops.*

Chile Pork Chops

This is a quick and easy dinner flavored with salsa and Hatch chiles, served over rice. The recipe works just as well with skinless, boneless chicken breasts.

2 T. olive oil
4 boneless pork chops
1 cup salsa
2 Hatch green chiles, roasted, peeled,
   stemmed, seeded, and chopped
2 cups cooked white rice, hot

Heat the oil in a 12-inch skillet over medium-high heat. Add the pork and brown it on both sides.

Stir in the salsa and chiles. Bring to a boil, then reduce the heat and simmer for 30 minutes, stirring and turning the pork chops occasionally. Serve over rice.

Perfect Pork

Pork and Hatch chiles are perfect together.

2 T. olive oil
1 pound lean pork, cut into 1/4-inch pieces
1 red bell pepper, stemmed, seeded,
   and chopped
5 Hatch green chiles, roasted, peeled,
   stemmed, seeded, and chopped
1/2 cup chopped green onion
1 garlic clove, minced
1 tsp. ground cumin
1 tsp. chili powder
1/2 cup water
2 T. all-purpose flour
Salt and freshly ground black pepper
3 cups cooked white rice, hot
1/2 cup shredded Cheddar cheese
1/2 cup sour cream

Heat the oil in a 12-inch skillet over medium-high heat. Add the pork and brown it on all sides. Remove and set aside.

Reduce the heat to medium. Add the bell pepper to the skillet. Sauté until tender. Add the chiles, onion, and garlic. Sauté for one more minute.

Add the cumin, chili powder, and water. Sprinkle the flour over and stir to mix until thickened.

Return the meat to the skillet. Cook, stirring occasionally, for 10 minutes or until the pork is cooked through and the vegetables are tender, adding more water if necessary. Season with salt and pepper to taste.

Serve over rice. Top with cheese and a dollop of sour cream.

Pork and Veggies

This stew has practically everything you could ever want in a meal. Feel free to vary the ingredients, adding whatever you like.

2 T. olive oil
2 pounds pork tenderloin, cut into cubes
2 large onions, chopped
1 red bell pepper, chopped
3 garlic cloves, minced
1 cup Hatch green chiles, roasted, peeled,
   stemmed, seeded, and chopped
2 cups chicken broth
4 medium Yukon Gold potatoes, cut into cubes
3 carrots, sliced
2 large tomatoes, chopped
1 cup sliced fresh green beans
1 cup frozen corn, thawed
1 cup black beans, cooked
1 tsp. dried cumin
Salt and freshly ground black pepper

Heat the oil in a Dutch oven over medium-high heat. Add the pork and brown it on all sides. Remove and set aside.

Add the onions and bell pepper to the pan. Sauté until tender. Add the garlic and chiles. Sauté for one more minute.

Return the meat to the skillet. Add the broth. Bring to a boil, then reduce the heat and simmer for one hour, stirring occasionally.

Add the potatoes, carrots, tomatoes, green beans, corn, and black beans. Season with the cumin, and the salt and pepper to taste. Stir to mix and simmer for one more hour, stirring occasionally.

Pork Fajitas

If you want fajitas in a flash, this recipe only takes about 20 minutes. Use fresh Hatch chiles—not roasted—stemmed, seeded, and sliced.

> 1-1/4 pounds pork loin, cut into strips
> 1 T. fajita seasoning
> 2/3 cup bottled Italian dressing
>   or tequila lime marinade
> 2 green bell peppers, cut into strips
> 2 red bell peppers, cut into strips
> 4 Hatch green chiles, cut into strips
> 1 large onion, cut into slices
> Flour tortillas, warmed
> Refried beans and rice
> Sour cream and/or guacamole
> Cheddar or Monterey Jack cheese

Place the pork in a medium-size bowl. Sprinkle the fajita seasoning on both sides. Pour the dressing over the pork and stir to coat. Marinate for 10 minutes.

Heat a 12-inch skillet over medium-high heat. Add the pork and sauté until the meat begins to brown, then add the green and red bell peppers, the chiles, and onion. Cover and cook for 10 minutes or until the vegetables are tender, stirring occasionally.

Serve with warm flour tortillas and various accompaniments, such as refried beans, rice, and sour cream or guacamole. Top with cheese, if desired.

This is also a great recipe for chicken or beef fajitas.

Chicken

Cheesy Chile Chicken Cutlets

I threw this together one night with just a few ingredients.
It turned out to be absolutely delicious.

4 skinless, boneless chicken breasts,
   pounded thin and cut in half
1/4 T. black pepper
1/4 T. ground cumin
1/2 T. Mexican oregano, crumbled
1/4 T. chili powder
1 small onion, diced
1/4 tsp. salt
2 garlic cloves, finely chopped
1 (14.5 oz.) can diced tomatoes
4 Hatch green chiles, roasted, peeled,
   stemmed, seeded, and cut in half
8 slices Asadero cheese (or substitute
   Monterey Jack cheese)

Lightly spray a 12-inch skillet with nonstick cooking spray. Heat over medium-high heat.

Add the chicken and brown it on both sides. Season with the pepper, cumin, oregano, and chili powder while the chicken is cooking. Remove the chicken to a plate and set aside.

Add the onion and sprinkle with the salt. Sauté until tender. Add the garlic and sauté for one more minute.

Return the chicken to the skillet. Stir in the tomatoes. Bring to a boil, then reduce the heat, cover, and simmer for 15 minutes or until the chicken is cooked through, turning occasionally.

Place one slice of chile and cheese on each chicken cutlet. Cover and heat through until the cheese melts.

Asadero Chicken Bundles

This recipe comes from my good friend and fellow foodie blogger, Teresa, of Mexican-American Cooking.

6 slices Asadero cheese

3 Hatch green chiles, roasted, peeled,
   stemmed, seeded, and cut in half

6 skinless, boneless chicken breasts,
   pounded thin

1 cup dried bread crumbs (Panko)

1 T. McCormick's Mexican seasoning

2. T. butter

Chile Con Queso

2 T. bacon fat

1 small onion, chopped

2 Hatch green chiles, roasted, peeled,
   stemmed, seeded, and chopped

1 garlic clove, minced

2 large ripe tomatoes, peeled and finely chopped

2-1/2 cups shredded Jack or Longhorn cheese

Salt, to taste

2 green onions, sliced

Preheat the oven to 350 degrees. Lightly spray a 13 x 9 glass baking dish with nonstick cooking spray. Set aside.

Place one slice of cheese and one slice of chile on each chicken breast. Roll up and secure with a wooden toothpick.

Combine the bread crumbs and Mexican seasoning on a dinner plate. Coat the chicken on all sides in this mixture.

Melt the butter in a 12-inch skillet over medium-high heat. Add the chicken and brown it on all sides.

Place the chicken in the prepared baking dish and bake for 30 to 40 minutes.

While this is cooking, prepare the sauce. Heat the bacon fat in a 12-inch skillet over medium heat. Add the onion. Sauté until tender. Add the chiles and garlic. Sauté for one more minute.

Add the tomatoes and cheese. Season with salt to taste. Heat until the sauce is hot and the cheese melts, stirring occasionally.

Remove the toothpicks and place the chicken on a plate. Cover with the sauce and garnish with green onions.

 If you don't have bacon fat, use butter to sauté the chiles and onion.

Chicken Capers

This comes together in practically no time in the microwave.

4 skinless, boneless chicken breasts,
   cooked and cut into bite-size pieces
1-1/2 T. capers
1/2 T. olive oil
1/3 cup water
Salt and freshly ground black pepper
1 medium onion, finely chopped
2 Hatch green chiles, roasted, peeled,
   stemmed, seeded, and chopped
3 garlic cloves, minced
5 green olives, seeded and chopped
3 cups cooked white rice, hot
1 lemon, cut into wedges

Combine all the ingredients except the rice and lemon in a large microwave-safe bowl. Cook on high for 10 minutes or until the onion is tender, stirring once halfway through cooking. Serve over rice with a lemon wedge on the side.

Cheddar Chicken

This quick and easy dinner is delicious. Chicken, black beans, and corn are a perfect combination.

2 tsp. chili powder
1/4 tsp. salt
1/4 tsp. black pepper
4 skinless, boneless chicken breasts
2 T. olive oil
1 (15 oz.) can black beans,
   drained and rinsed
1 cup frozen corn, thawed
4 Hatch green chiles, roasted, peeled,
   stemmed, seeded, and chopped
1/2 cup salsa
2 cups cooked white rice, hot
1/4 cup shredded Cheddar cheese
2 T. chopped cilantro

Combine the chili powder, salt, and pepper in a small bowl. Sprinkle this mixture over the chicken.

Heat the oil in a 12-inch skillet over medium-high heat. Add the chicken and brown it on both sides.

Add the beans, corn, chiles, and salsa. Stir to mix. Bring to a boil, then reduce the heat, cover, and simmer for 15 minutes or until the vegetables are tender and the chicken is cooked through, stirring occasionally.

Serve over rice. Sprinkle with cheese and cilantro.

 Cilantro has a strong, distinctive taste. If it's a bit too much for you, substitute parsley.

Tequila-Sauced Chicken

A really delicious take on Chicken Cordon Bleu.

   6 slices Pepper Jack cheese
   6 thin slices ham
   6 Hatch green chiles, roasted, peeled,
      stemmed, seeded, and cut open
   6 skinless, boneless chicken breasts,
      pounded thin
   4 T. butter, divided
   1 (16 oz.) container sliced mushrooms
   1 cup tequila
   1/2 cup heavy cream

Preheat the oven to 350 degrees. Lightly spray a 13 x 9 glass baking dish with nonstick cooking spray. Set aside.

Place one slice of cheese, one slice of ham, and one chile on each chicken breast. Roll up and secure with a wooden toothpick.

Melt half the butter in a 12-inch skillet over medium-high heat. Add the chicken and brown it on all sides.

Place the chicken in the prepared baking dish. Bake for 30 to 40 minutes.

About 15 minutes before serving, melt the remaining butter in the skillet over medium heat. Add the mushrooms and sauté for 5 minutes.

Add the tequila to the mushrooms and cook for 8 minutes to let the sauce reduce by one-half, stirring occasionally.

Stir in the heavy cream and cook until the sauce is slightly thickened. Add the chicken. Stir to coat with the cream sauce mixture.

Remove the toothpicks and place the chicken on a plate. Slice into 1/2-inch pinwheels. Cover with the sauce.

Cornmeal Chicken

Chicken, coated in a cornmeal crust, lends crunch to this recipe.

2 large eggs
2 T. water
1 cup yellow cornmeal
2 T. Parmesan cheese
1/2 tsp. ground cumin
1/2 tsp. chili powder
1/2 tsp. cayenne pepper
4 skinless, boneless chicken breasts
2 cups salsa
1 cup shredded Monterey Jack cheese
4 Hatch green chiles, roasted, peeled,
    stemmed, seeded, and chopped
3 cups cooked white rice, hot
1 (8 oz.) container sour cream

Preheat the oven to 425 degrees. Lightly spray a 13 x 9 glass baking dish with nonstick cooking spray. Set aside.

Whisk the eggs and water together in a small bowl.

Combine the cornmeal, Parmesan cheese, cumin, chili powder, and cayenne pepper on a dinner plate.

Dip the chicken breasts in the egg mixture, then dredge in the cornmeal mixture, coating evenly. Shake off the excess. Place the chicken in the prepared baking dish and bake for 30 to 35 minutes or until the juices run clear when pierced with a sharp knife.

Remove from the oven and pour the salsa over. Sprinkle with the cheese and chiles. Return to the oven and bake for 10 minutes or until the cheese melts.

Serve over rice with sour cream on the side.

Chile-Sauced Chicken

A cream cheese and chile sauce cover this chicken.

4 skinless, boneless chicken breasts
2 cups chicken broth
2 bay leaves
2 whole peppercorns
1 onion, coarsely chopped
3 celery stalks, coarsely chopped
2 carrots, coarsely chopped
2 tsp. ground cumin
1 (8 oz.) package cream cheese, softened
4 Hatch green chiles, roasted, peeled,
    stemmed, seeded, and chopped
4 T. butter
Salt and freshly ground black pepper

Place the chicken in a large saucepan. Add the broth, bay leaves, peppercorns, onion, celery, carrots, and cumin. Bring to a boil, then reduce the heat and simmer for 20 minutes or until the chicken is cooked through.

Remove the chicken and set aside. Drain, reserving the broth. Discard the bay leaves, peppercorns, onion, celery, and carrots. (These were used to season the chicken.)

Preheat the oven to 350 degrees. Lightly spray a 13 x 9 glass baking dish with nonstick cooking spray. Set aside.

Place the cream cheese, chiles, 1-1/2 cups of the reserved broth, and the butter in a blender. Blend until smooth and creamy. Season with salt and pepper to taste.

Place the chicken in the prepared baking dish. Pour the sauce over. Cover with aluminum foil and bake for 20 to 25 minutes.

Chicken Pasta Verde

A slice of Hatch chile heaven.

3 T. olive oil, divided
1 (16 oz.) container sliced mushrooms
1/3 cup diced onion
1 medium tomato, diced
1 (10 oz.) container heavy whipping cream
3 Hatch green chiles, roasted, peeled,
   stemmed, seeded, and chopped
Salt and freshly ground black pepper
1/2 cup grated Parmesan cheese, divided
2 skinless, boneless chicken breasts, grilled and sliced
1/4 cup diced red bell pepper
Spinach fettuccine pasta, cooked

Heat 2 T. of the oil in a 12-inch skillet over medium heat. Add the mushrooms and onion. Sauté until the onion is tender and the mushrooms are brown. Stir in the tomato. Remove to a plate and set aside.

Wipe out the skillet with a paper towel. Place the cream, mushroom mixture, chiles, salt and pepper to taste, and half the cheese into a cold skillet. Bring the mixture to a simmer, then reduce the heat as soon as it starts to bubble. Let simmer for 10 minutes or until the flavors are blended, stirring occasionally.

While this is cooking, heat the remaining oil in an 8-inch skillet over medium-high heat. Add the red bell pepper. Sauté until tender. Top the pasta with the chicken and the mushroom mixture. Garnish with the red bell pepper and remaining cheese.

You can buy pre-packaged sliced, grilled chicken breasts. Heat them before serving.

Tortilla Chip Chicken

Another easy, cheesy, delicious recipe. Just put all the ingredients together and toss them in the oven.

4 skinless, boneless chicken breasts
1/2 cup butter, melted
1 tsp. salt
1/4 tsp. black pepper
1/2 tsp. paprika
1-1/2 cups crushed tortilla chips
1 (10 oz.) can enchilada sauce
4 Hatch green chiles, roasted, peeled,
    stemmed, seeded, and chopped
1 cup shredded Cheddar cheese
1/2 cup green onion, chopped
1 (2.25 oz.) can sliced black olives

Preheat the oven to 375 degrees.

Place the chicken in a 13 x 9 glass baking dish. Pour the melted butter over the chicken. Sprinkle with the salt, pepper, and paprika. Cover with aluminum foil. Bake for 45 minutes, turning the chicken once during cooking.

Remove from the oven and sprinkle the chips over the chicken. Pour the enchilada sauce over. Top with the chiles, cheese, onion, and olives. Return to the oven for 10 minutes or until the cheese is melted.

Chicken Penne Skillet

Similar to mac 'n' cheese, this skillet dinner features penne pasta tossed with two kinds of cheese and mixed with a creamy tomatillo sauce, then topped with a crunchy cheese topping.

3/4 cup chicken broth
8 tomatillos, husked, rinsed,
    cored, and chopped
6 Hatch green chiles, roasted, peeled,
    stemmed, seeded, and chopped
1 medium onion, chopped
2 garlic cloves, minced
1/2 cup cilantro leaves
1 tsp. salt
2 T. butter
1-1/2 cups half-and-half
2 cups shredded Monterey Jack cheese
1 cup cubed white Cheddar cheese
1 (16 oz.) package penne pasta,
    cooked al dente and drained
2 cups shredded, cooked chicken
3/4 cup crushed tortilla chips
2 T. butter, melted
2 cups shredded Monterey Jack cheese

Place the broth, tomatillos, and chiles in a large saucepan. Heat over medium heat for 10 minutes.

Place the mixture in a food processor. Add the onion, garlic, cilantro, and salt. Blend until smooth.

Melt the butter in the same saucepan over medium heat. Add the tomatillo mixture. Cook for 5 minutes, stirring often.

Stir in the half-and-half, and the Monterey Jack and Cheddar cheeses. Cook just until the cheese is melted.

Add the pasta and chicken. Toss to mix. Place in an oven-proof skillet.

Combine the tortilla chips, melted butter, and the Monterey Jack cheese in a medium-size bowl. Spread this over the pasta and chicken. Place the skillet under the broiler and cook for 10 minutes or until golden brown.

Salsa Chicken

Salsa, black beans, corn, and chicken make a perfect meal.

2 T. vegetable oil
4 skinless, boneless chicken breasts
1 T. chili powder
1/2 T. ground cumin
Salt and freshly ground black pepper
1 (10 oz.) jar thick and chunky salsa
1 (15 oz.) can black beans, drained and rinsed
4 Hatch green chiles, roasted, peeled,
    stemmed, seeded, and chopped
1 cup frozen corn, thawed
1/4 cup water
2 T. minced cilantro
2 cups cooked white rice, hot
1 cup shredded Cheddar cheese

Heat the oil in a 12-inch skillet over medium-high heat. Add the chicken and brown it on both sides. Sprinkle with chili powder, cumin, and the salt and pepper to taste while the chicken is cooking.

Stir in the salsa, beans, chiles, corn, water, and cilantro. Bring to a boil, then reduce the heat, cover, and simmer for 10 minutes, stirring occasionally.

Serve over rice. Sprinkle with cheese.

Tomatillo Chicken

A double dose of Hatch chiles. Stuffed with chicken, cheese, and chopped chiles, and served with a tomatillo sauce, these chiles are incredibly delicious.

> 8 tomatillos, husked, rinsed,
>   cored, and chopped
> 4 garlic cloves, chopped
> 1 medium onion, quartered
> 1/2 bunch cilantro, chopped
> 2 Hatch green chiles, roasted, peeled,
>   stemmed, seeded, and chopped
> 1/2 tsp. salt
> 1/2 tsp. black pepper
> 2 T. extra virgin olive oil
> 1/2 cup water
> 3 cups chopped, cooked chicken
> 8 Hatch green chiles, cut open and seeded
> 1 (8 oz.) brick Monterey Jack
>   cheese, cut into one-inch strips

Place the tomatillos, garlic, onion, cilantro, two chopped chiles, the salt, pepper, oil, and water into a blender or a food processor. Purée until smooth.

Place the mixture into a medium-size saucepan. Bring to a boil, then reduce the heat and simmer for 20 minutes, stirring occasionally. Remove the pan from the heat and set aside to cool.

Preheat the oven to 325 degrees. Lightly spray a 13 x 9 glass baking dish with nonstick cooking spray. Set aside.

Mix the chicken with one cup of the tomatillo sauce in a medium-size bowl. Stuff the mixture into the whole chiles and place them in the prepared baking dish. Place the cheese strips on top of the chicken. Fold the chile over to cover the cheese.

Bake for 20 to 25 minutes or until the cheese is bubbly and the chiles are nicely browned. Warm the remaining tomatillo sauce and serve over the stuffed chiles.

Ranchero Chicken

This is similar to Chicken Parmesan, topped with Cheddar cheese and served over rice instead of pasta.

2 T. olive oil
4 skinless, boneless chicken breasts
1 medium onion, chopped
3 Hatch green chiles, roasted, peeled,
    stemmed, seeded, and chopped
2 cups salsa
Salt and freshly ground black pepper
2 cups cooked white rice, hot
1/2 cup shredded Cheddar cheese
2 green onions, sliced

Heat the oil in a 12-inch skillet over medium-high heat. Add the chicken and brown it on both sides. Remove and set aside.

Reduce the heat to medium. Add the onion and chiles to the skillet, adding more oil if necessary. Sauté until tender.

Stir in the salsa. Return the chicken to the skillet. Bring to a boil, then reduce the heat, cover, and simmer for 20 minutes, stirring and turning the chicken occasionally. Season with salt and pepper to taste. Serve over rice. Sprinkle with cheese and top with the onions.

Mesilla Chicken

Just like the Mesilla Valley, where the Hatch chiles are grown, this recipe offers you a starting point to grow your chicken recipe into a delicious Hatch dinner. Just add a side of rice and beans.

2 T. vegetable oil

2 tsp. paprika

1/2 tsp. cayenne pepper

1 tsp. ground cumin

1 tsp. salt

1 tsp. black pepper

4 skinless, boneless chicken breasts

2 garlic cloves, minced

1 medium onion, finely chopped

4 Hatch green chiles, roasted, peeled,
stemmed, seeded, and chopped

3/4 cup chicken broth

2 T. all-purpose flour

2 T. water

4 cilantro sprigs

Heat the oil in a 12-inch skillet over medium-high heat. Add the paprika, cayenne pepper, cumin, salt, and pepper. Stir to mix. Add the chicken and brown it on both sides.

Add the garlic, onion, chiles, and broth. Stir to mix. Bring to a boil, then reduce the heat, cover, and simmer for 45 minutes, stirring occasionally.

Remove the chicken to a plate and set aside. Keep warm.

Whisk the flour and water together in a small bowl. Add this mixture to the skillet and cook, stirring constantly, until the sauce is thickened.

Pour the sauce over the chicken. Garnish with a cilantro sprig.

Cruces Chicken

Topped with bacon and chiles, then smothered in cheese.

1 cup bread crumbs
1 tsp. salt
1 tsp. black pepper
4 skinless, boneless chicken breasts
2 T. vegetable oil
4 slices thick-cut bacon, cooked
2 Hatch green chiles, roasted, peeled,
    stemmed, seeded, and cut in half
1 cup shredded Asadero cheese

Preheat the oven to 375 degrees. Lightly spray a 13 x 9 glass baking dish with nonstick cooking spray. Set aside.

Combine the bread crumbs, salt, and pepper on a dinner plate. Dredge the chicken breasts in the bread crumb mixture.

Heat the oil in a 12-inch skillet over medium-high heat. Add the chicken and brown it on both sides.

Place the chicken in the prepared baking dish and bake for 15 minutes or until the chicken is cooked through.

Remove from the oven and top each chicken breast with one slice of bacon and a slice of chile. Cover with cheese and return to the oven for 5 minutes or until the cheese is melted.

You may substitute Monterey Jack cheese for the Asadero cheese.

Crunchy Chicken Olé

Olé... Oh, yeah!

1/4 cup butter, divided
1 medium red onion, finely chopped
4 Hatch green chiles, roasted, peeled,
    stemmed, seeded, and chopped
1 cup shredded Monterey Jack cheese
1/2 cup shredded Cheddar cheese
1 T. chopped cilantro
6 skinless, boneless chicken
    breasts, pounded thin
2 tsp. ground cumin
1 tsp. chili powder
1 cup crushed Fritos

Preheat the oven to 350 degrees. Lightly spray a 13 x 9 glass baking dish with nonstick cooking spray. Set aside.

Melt 2 T. of the butter in a 12-inch skillet over medium heat. Add the onion and chiles. Sauté until the onion is tender.

Combine the Monterey Jack and Cheddar cheeses, the sautéed onion and chiles, and the cilantro in a medium-size bowl.

Place equal amounts of the mixture on each chicken breast. Roll up and secure with a wooden toothpick. Place seam side down in the prepared baking dish.

Melt the remaining butter in a small bowl in the microwave. Stir in the cumin and chili powder. Pour the butter mixture over the chicken. Cover with aluminum foil and bake for 45 minutes.

Remove from the oven and uncover. Top with the crushed Fritos. Return to the oven and bake for 5 more minutes. Remove the toothpicks before serving.

Catch-All Chicken

This recipe has all the ingredients for a delicious dinner.
Top with shredded Cheddar cheese.

2 skinless, boneless chicken breasts
1 (1.25 oz.) package taco seasoning mix
3 T. water
2 T. vegetable oil
1 medium onion, coarsely chopped
3 Hatch green chiles, roasted, peeled,
   stemmed, seeded, and chopped
1 cup frozen corn, thawed
1 (2 oz.) jar pimientos, drained
1 (15 oz.) can black beans,
   drained and rinsed
3 cups cooked white rice, hot
1 cup picante sauce

Place the chicken in a medium-size saucepan and cover
with water. Bring to a boil, then reduce the heat and simmer for
15 minutes or until the chicken is cooked through. Remove to a
cutting board, let cool slightly, then coarsely chop the chicken.

Mix the taco seasoning and water in a medium-size bowl.
Add the chicken and stir to coat. Set aside.

Heat the oil in a 12-inch skillet over medium-high heat.
Add the onion, chiles, and corn. Sauté until tender. Add the
pimientos, beans, chicken, rice, and picante sauce. Stir to mix
and heat through.

 *You can substitute one (6 oz.) package Southwest
seasoned chicken breasts for the chopped chicken
and taco seasoning.*

Arroz Con Pollo

Arroz con Pollo means chicken and rice. You'll also find sausage and Hatch chiles in this recipe.

> 2 T. vegetable oil
> 6 skinless, boneless chicken breasts,
>   cut into bite-size pieces
> 1 pound mild Italian sausage, cut
>   into one-inch chunks
> 1 medium onion, chopped
> 4 Hatch green chiles, roasted, peeled,
>   stemmed, seeded, and chopped
> 2 garlic cloves, minced
> 1 cup long grain white rice
> 1 tsp. dried oregano
> 1/2 tsp. paprika
> 1 cup chicken broth
> 1/2 cup dry white wine
> Salt and freshly ground black pepper

Heat the oil in a Dutch oven over medium-high heat. Add the chicken and brown it on both sides. Remove and set aside.

Add the sausage and onion to the pan. Sauté until the sausage is cooked and the onion is tender. Add the chiles and garlic. Sauté for one more minute. Drain. Remove the mixture and set aside.

Add the rice, oregano, and paprika. Stir until the rice is coated with the spice mixture.

Add the broth and wine. Return the chicken and the sausage mixture to the pan. Bring to a boil, then reduce the heat, cover, and simmer for 30 minutes or until the rice is tender and most of the liquid is absorbed, stirring occasionally. Season with salt and pepper to taste.

Chile Stuffed Chicken

*This is a basic recipe that you can get really creative with.
Add pimientos, sun-dried tomatoes, chopped bacon, pine nuts,
chopped black olives, or diced green onions into the stuffing.*

1 (8 oz.) brick Monterey Jack cheese,
  cut into 12 strips
3 Hatch green chiles, roasted, peeled,
  stemmed, seeded, and cut in half
6 skinless, boneless chicken breasts,
  pounded thin
1/4 cup chicken broth
1/4 tsp. paprika

Preheat the oven to 350 degrees. Lightly spray a 13 x 9 glass
baking dish with nonstick cooking spray. Set aside.

Place two cheese strips and one slice of chile on each chicken
breast. Roll up and secure with a wooden toothpick.

Place seam side down in the prepared baking dish. Pour the
broth over. Bake for 20 minutes, basting once or twice. Remove
the toothpicks and sprinkle with paprika before serving.

*Instead of using Monterey Jack, use Asadero cheese
instead. It's a Mexican white cheese, which melts
well and has a creamy texture.*

Chicken Rolls

Stuffed with cream cheese, green onions, and chiles with a touch of cumin, then covered in salsa, these chicken rolls are juicy and delicious.

1 (16 oz.) jar salsa, divided
1 (8 oz.) package cream cheese, softened
3 Hatch green chiles, roasted, peeled,
    stemmed, seeded, and chopped
2 tsp. ground cumin
4 green onions, chopped, divided
6 skinless, boneless chicken
    breasts, pounded thin
1 cup shredded Cheddar cheese
6 cilantro sprigs

Preheat the oven to 350 degrees. Place 4 to 5 T. of the salsa in a 13 x 9 glass baking dish to cover the bottom. Set aside.

Beat the cream cheese until smooth in a medium-size bowl.

Stir in the chiles, cumin, and three-fourths of the onions. Place equal amounts of the cream cheese mixture on each chicken breast. Roll up and secure with a wooden toothpick. Place seam side down in the prepared baking dish. Spoon the remaining cream cheese mixture and the remaining salsa over the chicken rolls. Cover with aluminum foil and bake for 30 minutes.

Remove from the oven, uncover, and sprinkle the cheese over the top. Return to the oven and bake for 10 more minutes or until the cheese is melted.

Spoon equal amounts of the salsa, from the baking dish, on dinner plates in a swirling pattern. Remove the toothpicks and place a chicken roll on top. Garnish with the remaining onions. Place a sprig of cilantro on the side.

Chicken Chile Casserole

This casserole has it all in one dish—chicken, brown rice,
and beans, topped with a glorious layer of melted cheese.

4 skinless, boneless chicken
   breasts, cut into strips
1 T. chili powder, or more to taste
1 cup quick-cooking brown rice
1 cup chicken broth, to prepare the rice
1 (15 oz.) can black beans, drained and rinsed
2 Hatch green chiles, roasted, peeled,
   stemmed, seeded, and chopped
1/8 tsp. ground cumin
1/8 tsp. cayenne pepper
1/8 tsp. garlic powder
1/4 tsp. onion powder
1/4 tsp. dried oregano
1 cup shredded Cheddar cheese

Preheat the oven to 350 degrees. Lightly spray a 13 x 9 glass baking dish with nonstick cooking spray.

Place the chicken in the prepared baking dish. Sprinkle with the chili powder. Bake for 20 minutes.

While the chicken is cooking, prepare the rice according to the package directions, except substitute chicken broth for the water. When the rice is done, remove the pan from the heat and mix in the beans, chiles, cumin, cayenne pepper, garlic powder, onion powder, and oregano.

Remove the baking dish from the oven and stir the chicken strips. Spoon the drippings from the cooked chicken into the rice mixture. Stir well, then spoon the rice mixture over the chicken and stir to mix. Top with the cheese. Return to the oven for 10 minutes to melt the cheese.

Chicken and Corn Tortilla Casserole

If you're wondering what to do with leftover chicken and stale tortillas, this tasty casserole featuring a sour cream sauce makes a quick, weeknight dinner. You can also use a rotisserie chicken, cut up, and tortilla chips.

1-1/2 cups chicken broth
1 cup milk
1/2 cup all-purpose flour
1 (8 oz.) container sour cream
1 (14.5 oz.) can diced tomatoes
3 Hatch green chiles, roasted, peeled,
   stemmed, seeded, and chopped
1/4 cup chopped cilantro
1 T. chili powder
1 tsp. dried oregano
1/2 tsp. ground cumin
1-1/2 tsp. olive oil
1 large onion, chopped
2 garlic cloves, minced
10 (6-inch) corn tortillas, cut in quarters
2 cups diced, cooked chicken
1/2 cup shredded Cheddar cheese

Preheat the oven to 375 degrees. Bring the broth to a simmer in a medium-size saucepan.

Whisk the milk and flour together in a small bowl to make a paste. Add the paste to the broth and cook for 3 minutes, whisking constantly, until the broth is thickened and smooth. Remove the pan from the heat and stir in the sour cream, tomatoes, chiles, cilantro, chili powder, oregano, and cumin. Set aside.

Heat the oil in a 12-inch skillet over medium-high heat. Add the onion. Sauté until the onion is tender-crisp. Add the garlic and sauté for one more minute.

Line the bottom of a 13 x 9 glass baking dish with half the tortillas. Top with half the chicken and half the onion mixture. Spoon half the sauce over the top. Repeat with the remaining tortillas, chicken, onion mixture, and sauce. Sprinkle with the cheese and bake for 25 to 30 minutes.

Chicken Fiesta

A Fiesta is a party and you'll feel like celebrating when you enjoy this dish.

1/2 cup butter, melted
2 cups finely crushed Fritos
2 T. taco seasoning
4 skinless, boneless chicken breasts
2 T. butter
4 Hatch green chiles, roasted, peeled, stemmed, seeded, and chopped
1 tsp. chicken bouillon granules
2 cups heavy cream
1 cup shredded Monterey Jack cheese
1 cup shredded sharp Cheddar cheese
1 T. paprika

Preheat the oven to 350 degrees. Pour the melted butter into a 13 x 9 glass baking dish. Set aside.

Combine the Fritos and the taco seasoning on a dinner plate. Dredge the chicken in the Fritos mixture, coating it well on both sides. Place the chicken in the prepared baking dish.

Melt the 2 T. butter in a 12-inch skillet over medium-low heat. Stir in the chiles, bouillon, cream and the Monterey Jack and Cheddar cheeses. Stir until the cheese is melted. Pour the sauce over the chicken. Sprinkle with paprika. Bake for 55 minutes.

Tortilla Chip Chicken Casserole

Flavored with chiles, and topped with tortilla chips, this casserole is quick and easy.

  4 skinless, boneless chicken breasts
  1 (10 oz.) can chicken broth
  2 (14.5 oz.) cans diced tomatoes
  1 medium onion, coarsely chopped
  2 garlic cloves
  3 Hatch green chiles, roasted, peeled,
    stemmed, seeded, and chopped
  1/4 cup chopped cilantro
  Salt and freshly ground black pepper
  8 cups coarsely crushed tortilla chips
  1-1/2 cups shredded Monterey Jack cheese
  1 (8 oz.) container sour cream

Place the chicken and broth in a medium-size saucepan. Bring to a boil, then reduce the heat and simmer for 15 minutes or until the chicken is cooked through. Remove the chicken to a cutting board, let cool slightly, then shred it with two forks. Set aside. Reserve the broth.

Preheat the oven to 425 degrees. Lightly spray a 13 x 9 glass baking dish with nonstick cooking spray. Set aside.

Place the tomatoes, onion, garlic, and chiles in a blender. Purée until smooth. Pour the tomato mixture into a medium-size saucepan. Simmer over medium-low heat for 5 minutes or until slightly thickened. Add the chicken, reserved broth, and cilantro. Heat through. Season with salt and pepper to taste.

Place half the tortilla chips in the prepared baking dish. Top with half the tomato-chicken mixture and half the cheese. Repeat.

Bake for 15 minutes or until the cheese begins to brown. Serve with sour cream on the side.

Seafood

Chile Cod

Seasoned with salsa, coated with corn chips, and topped with Hatch chiles.

 1-1/2 pounds cod fillets
 1 cup salsa
 1 cup shredded Cheddar cheese
 1/2 cup crushed corn chips
 1/4 cup sour cream
 1 avocado, peeled, pitted, and sliced
 2 Hatch green chiles, roasted, peeled,
    stemmed, seeded, and chopped

Preheat the oven to 400 degrees. Lightly spray a 13 x 9 glass baking dish with nonstick cooking spray.

Place the fillets in the prepared baking dish. Cover each fillet with salsa and cheese. Top with corn chips. Bake for 15 minutes or until the fish flakes easily when tested with a fork.

Top each fillet with sour cream, avocado slices, and chiles.

Hacienda Halibut

Quick and easy, salsa-seasoned fillets.

1 (16 oz.) package frozen halibut fillets
2 T. butter, melted
2 Hatch green chiles, roasted, peeled,
  stemmed, seeded, and chopped
1 (8 oz.) jar thick and chunky salsa
1 (2.25 oz.) can sliced black olives
2 green onions, chopped (optional)
1 avocado, peeled, pitted, and chopped

Preheat the oven to 350 degrees.

Place the frozen fillets in a 13 x 9 glass baking dish. Cover with aluminum foil and bake for 25 minutes.

Remove from the oven and uncover. Pour the melted butter over each fillet. Top with the chiles, then spoon the salsa over. Sprinkle the olives over the salsa.

Return to the oven and bake for 15 more minutes or until the fish flakes easily when tested with a fork. Remove from the oven and top with the onions. Serve with avocado on the side.

Hatch Halibut

This is baked and served with a creamy chile sauce.

2 T. butter
1 medium onion, diced
4 Hatch green chiles, roasted, peeled,
    stemmed, seeded, and chopped
1 garlic clove, minced
1/2 cup half-and-half
1 pound halibut fillets
Salt and freshly ground black pepper

Preheat the oven to 375 degrees. Lightly spray a 13 x 9 glass baking dish with nonstick cooking spray. Set aside.

Melt the butter in a 12-inch skillet over medium heat. Add the onion and sauté until tender.

Add the chiles and garlic. Sauté for one more minute.

Reduce the heat to low. Stir in the half-and-half. Simmer for 5 minutes to let the sauce reduce, stirring occasionally.

Place the fish in the prepared baking dish. Season with salt and pepper to taste. Spoon the sauce over the fish. Bake for 15 minutes or until the fish flakes easily when tested with a fork.

Grilled Flounder

Heat up the grill. There are all sorts of deliciousness in this recipe... eggplant, chiles, green onions, tomatoes, and wine.

1 lemon, cut in half
3 T. butter, divided
3 T. olive oil, divided
4 flounder fillets
1 cup diced eggplant
3 Hatch green chiles, roasted, peeled,
   stemmed, seeded, and chopped
1/4 cup chopped green onion
2 garlic cloves, mashed
1 cup diced tomato
1/2 cup white wine
1/2 tsp. salt
1/4 tsp. black pepper
1 T. chopped cilantro

Juice one-half of the lemon into a small bowl or cup. Cut the remaining half into slices and set both aside.

Heat 1 T. each of the butter and oil in a 12-inch skillet over low heat. Stir and set aside to let cool. When cool, dip the fillets into the butter mixture one at a time, coating all sides thoroughly. Place the fillets on a plate.

Preheat the barbecue grill.

Add the remaining butter and oil to the skillet. Heat over medium-high heat. Add the eggplant. Sauté for 5 minutes.

Add the chiles, onion, garlic, and tomato. Sauté for 2 more minutes. Add the wine and bring to a boil, then reduce the heat and simmer for 10 minutes. Season with the salt and pepper.

While this is cooking, oil the grill or place the fish in an oiled, hinged wire fish basket and grill for 4 to 5 minutes on each side. Remove to a serving platter.

Add the reserved lemon juice to the skillet. Stir and heat through, then spoon the mixture over the fish. Garnish with cilantro. Serve with lemon slices on the side.

Ceviche

Prepare this the night before you plan to serve it.

10 limes, juiced
1 pound firm white fish, finely chopped
1 large tomato, chopped
1/2 cup chopped black olives
2 T. fresh oregano, crushed
1/2 medium red onion, chopped
3 Hatch green chiles, roasted, peeled,
    stemmed, seeded, and chopped
1/2 tsp. salt
1/4 tsp. black pepper
1/4 to 1/2 cup olive oil
2 T. finely chopped cilantro

Juice the limes into a medium-size glass bowl. Add the fish and turn to coat with the juice. Cover and refrigerate overnight.

When ready to prepare, remove the fish from the refrigerator. Drain in a colander and return to the glass bowl.

Add the tomato, olives, oregano, onion, chiles, salt, and pepper one at a time, lightly tossing with olive oil. Garnish with cilantro.

Tequila Salmon

Who says tequila has to be mixed into a drink? It adds flavor to this dish.

3 T. olive oil, divided
1 small onion, finely chopped
2/3 cup water
Grated zest and juice of one lime
1/2 cup light cream
3 Hatch green chiles, roasted, peeled,
   stemmed, seeded, and chopped
Salt and freshly ground black pepper
3 T. tequila
4 salmon fillets
1 avocado, peeled, pitted, and sliced

Heat 1 T. of the oil in a 12-inch skillet over medium-high heat. Add the onion and sauté until tender. Add the water, lime zest, and lime juice. Cook for 8 to 10 minutes or until the sauce begins to reduce.

Reduce the heat to low. Slowly stir in the cream, then add the chiles. Cook, stirring constantly, for 2 to 3 minutes. Season with salt and pepper to taste.

Stir in the tequila. Turn off the heat and cover to keep warm.

Brush the top of the salmon fillets with 1 T. of the oil.

Heat a separate 12-inch skillet over high heat. Add the salmon, oiled side down. Cook for 2 to 3 minutes or until the underside is golden, then brush the top with the remaining 1 T. of the oil. Turn each fillet over and cook the other side until the fish flakes easily when tested with a fork.

Spoon the tequila sauce on four dinner plates. Place the fish on top of the sauce, then top with avocado slices.

Seafood Fajitas

There's something fishy about these fajitas...

1 garlic clove, minced
1/8 tsp. paprika
1/8 tsp. black pepper
1 T. fresh lime juice
1/4 tsp. cayenne pepper
2 tsp. Worcestershire sauce
1-1/2 pounds firm white fish fillets
2 T. vegetable oil, divided
1 small red onion, sliced
4 Hatch green chiles, roasted, peeled,
 stemmed, seeded, and chopped
1 (4 oz.) jar roasted red bell pepper,
 drained and chopped
8 (8-inch) flour tortillas, warmed
1 cup picante sauce
Guacamole (page 17)
1/2 cup shredded Monterey Jack cheese

Combine the garlic, paprika, pepper, lime juice, cayenne pepper, and Worcestershire sauce in a medium-size bowl. Add the fish and marinate in the refrigerator for 30 minutes.

Heat 1 T. of the oil in a 12-inch skillet over medium heat. Add the onion and sauté until tender. Stir in the chiles and bell pepper. Heat through. Remove and set aside.

Heat the remaining oil in the skillet. Remove the fish from the marinade and coarsely chop. Add the fish to the skillet and cook for 8 minutes or until the fish flakes easily when tested with a fork. Place the fish on a serving platter. Place the vegetables on the side. Serve with warm tortillas, picante sauce, guacamole, and cheese.

Sassy Snapper Stew

Sassy and spicy.

2 T. butter
1 medium red onion, chopped
4 Hatch green chiles, roasted, peeled,
    stemmed, seeded, and chopped
3 garlic cloves, finely minced
2 pounds red snapper fillets, cut
    into two-inch pieces
2 medium tomatoes, chopped
1/4 tsp. ground cumin
1/4 cup chopped cilantro
1 tsp. dried oregano
4 T. fresh lime juice
2 cups water
1/2 tsp. salt
1/4 tsp. black pepper
2 bay leaves

Melt the butter in a large saucepan over medium heat. Add the onion and sauté until tender. Add the chiles and garlic. Sauté for one more minute.

Add the fish, tomatoes, cumin, cilantro, oregano, lime juice, water, salt, pepper, and bay leaves. Bring to a boil, then reduce the heat, cover, and simmer for one hour, stirring occasionally. Remove the bay leaves before serving.

Crab Cakes

These are so good you might want to double the recipe.

1 pound jumbo lump crab meat,
   picked over to remove cartilage or shells
4 Hatch green chiles, roasted, peeled,
   stemmed, seeded, and chopped
3 green onions, minced
1 T. chopped fresh parsley
1-1/2 tsp. Old Bay seasoning
4 T. plain bread crumbs
1/4 cup mayonnaise
Salt and freshly ground black pepper
1 large egg, lightly beaten
2 cups panko bread crumbs
1/4 cup vegetable oil

Gently mix the crab meat, chiles, onions, parsley, the seasoning, the plain bread crumbs, and the mayonnaise in a medium-size bowl. Season with salt and pepper to taste.

Gently fold in the egg until the mixture clings together. Form into patties of equal size and thickness and place them on a dinner plate. Cover with plastic wrap and refrigerate for 30 minutes.

When ready to cook, place the panko bread crumbs on a dinner plate. Dredge the crab cakes in the panko, shaking off any excess. You may have to pack the panko on to adhere if the crab cakes are very cold.

Heat the oil in a large skillet. Fry the crab cakes for 4 minutes per side or until the outsides are crisp and browned. Drain on paper towels.

Crabby Chiles

These chiles may be crabby, but they are oh-so-delicious sitting on a bed of creamy corn and onions.

1 (4 oz.) package cream cheese, softened
1-1/2 cups shredded Monterey Jack cheese
2 T. Dijon mustard
1 T. fresh lime juice
Salt and freshly ground black pepper
6 oz. lump crab meat
4 Hatch green chiles, roasted, peeled,
   stemmed, seeded, and cut open
Sour Cream Corn Sauce
   3 T. butter
   1/3 cup chopped onion
   1 cup frozen corn, thawed
   1/2 cup half-and-half
   1/2 cup sour cream

Combine the cream cheese, Monterey Jack cheese, mustard, lime juice, and the salt and pepper to taste in a medium-size bowl.

Add the crab meat and gently mix, being careful not to break up the crab meat. Stuff the mixture into the chiles. Place the stuffed chiles in a 13 x 9 glass baking dish and refrigerate for 30 minutes.

When ready to cook, preheat the oven to 350 degrees. Bake for 20 minutes or until the stuffing is melted and hot.

While this is cooking, make the Sour Cream Corn Sauce. Melt the butter in a 12-inch skillet over medium heat. Add the onion and corn. Sauté until tender.

Reduce the heat to low. Stir in the half-and-half and the sour cream. Simmer for 5 minutes or until heated through. Spoon the sauce on dinner plates. Top with the crabby chiles.

Shrimp Stuffed Rellenos

These rellenos are baked in the oven. Use unroasted whole Hatch chiles.

1 T. butter
3 T. minced onion
3 T. minced celery
2 medium eggs, beaten
1 cup bread crumbs
1/2 cup milk
1 tsp. salt
1/4 tsp. black pepper
1 T. Worcestershire sauce
2 cups chopped, cooked shrimp
6 whole Hatch green chiles

Preheat the oven to 350 degrees. Lightly spray a 13 x 9 glass baking dish with nonstick cooking spray. Set aside.

Melt the butter in a 12-inch skillet over medium heat. Add the onion and celery. Sauté until tender.

Combine the eggs, bread crumbs, milk, salt, pepper, and Worcestershire sauce in a medium-size bowl. Add the sautéed vegetables and the shrimp. Stir to mix well.

Cut a slit halfway down the center of each chile. Do not cut through. Remove the seeds and stuff the shrimp mixture into the chiles. Seal with toothpicks if they start to fall apart. Place seam side down in the prepared baking dish. Cover with aluminum foil and bake for 20 to 25 minutes or until the chiles are softened and the stuffing is heated through.

If you'd like a firmer filling, chop the shrimp to a paste in a food processor.

Shrimp Cotija Chiles

Chiles stuffed with shrimp and spinach, seasoned with crushed red pepper and mixed with Cotija cheese, then drizzled with crema.

4 cups fresh spinach, washed
2 T. olive oil
1-1/2 pounds shrimp, peeled and deveined
3 garlic cloves, minced
3 cups grated Cotija cheese
2 tsp. chili powder
Zest and juice of one lemon
1 tsp. crushed red pepper flakes
Salt and freshly ground black pepper
8 Hatch green chiles, roasted, peeled,
    stemmed, seeded, and cut open
Mexican crema

Preheat the oven to 375 degrees. Lightly spray a 13 x 9 glass baking dish with nonstick cooking spray. Set aside.

Heat a 12-inch skillet over medium heat. Add the spinach, in batches, and cook until it wilts. Remove and set aside.

Wipe out the skillet and add the oil. When the oil is hot, add the shrimp and garlic. Cook until the shrimp are opaque.

Add the cheese, chili powder, lemon zest and juice, red pepper flakes, and the wilted spinach. Season with salt and pepper to taste. Stir to mix, then stuff the chiles with this mixture. Close the chiles to cover the filling. Place in the prepared baking dish. Bake for 20 minutes or until heated through. Drizzle with crema and serve.

If you can't find Cotija cheese, substitute another crumbly cheese, such as feta. You can use sour cream instead of the crema if you prefer.

Saucy Shrimp

This recipe has the perfect amount of seasoning and heat from the Hatch chiles.

2 large tomatoes
2 T. butter
1 T. olive oil
1 medium red onion, chopped
1 red bell pepper, chopped
2 Hatch green chiles, roasted, peeled,
   stemmed, seeded, and chopped
2 garlic cloves, minced
Salt and freshly ground black pepper
1 pound shrimp, peeled and deveined
2 cups cooked white rice, hot
1 lime, cut into wedges
1/4 cup chopped cilantro

Preheat the broiler. Place the tomatoes in a shallow baking pan about 5 inches from the heat. Broil for 5 minutes, then turn over and broil the other side for 3 minutes. Remove and let cool, then core, peel, and coarsely chop the tomatoes, reserving the juices. Set aside.

Melt the butter with the oil in a 12-inch skillet over medium-high heat. Add the onion and bell pepper. Sauté until tender. Add the chiles and garlic. Sauté for one more minute.

Stir in the reserved tomatoes with their juices. Season with salt and pepper to taste. Cover, reduce the heat, and simmer for 15 minutes, stirring occasionally.

Stir in the shrimp. Cover and simmer for 5 more minutes. Serve over rice with a lime wedge on the side. Garnish with cilantro.

Southwest Shrimp

Served over rice and topped with a chile-lime salsa, this shrimp has all the flavors of the Southwest.

1 pound shrimp, peeled, and
    deveined, with tails intact
Butter flavor nonstick cooking spray
Juice of 2 limes, divided
1 tsp. chili powder
Salt and freshly ground black pepper
2 T. butter
1 cup finely chopped red onion
3 Hatch green chiles, roasted, peeled,
    stemmed, seeded, and chopped
1 large ripe tomato, peeled, seeded
    and finely chopped
1/4 cup finely chopped cilantro
2 cups cooked white rice, hot

Place the shrimp in a medium-size bowl. Lightly spray them with the butter flavor nonstick cooking spray. Add half the lime juice, sprinkle with the chili powder, and season with the salt and pepper to taste. Toss to coat. Set aside.

Melt the butter in a 12-inch skillet over medium-high heat. Add the onion and chiles. Sauté for 2 minutes or until the onion is tender. Add the shrimp and sauté for 2 minutes or until they are opaque in the center. Stir in the tomato, cilantro, and remaining lime juice. Cook for one more minute. Serve over rice.

Breads and Tortillas

Basic Cornbread

Cornbread goes great with chili, as well as with soups and stews.

Butter, as needed, divided
1 cup yellow cornmeal
1-1/2 cups all-purpose flour
3/4 cup granulated sugar
4 tsp. baking powder
1 tsp. salt
1 cup milk
2 large eggs
2 Hatch green chiles, roasted, peeled,
   stemmed, seeded, and chopped
1/4 cup vegetable oil

Preheat the oven to 425 degrees. Lightly butter a 13 x 9 glass baking dish. Set aside.

Combine the cornmeal, flour, sugar, baking powder, salt, milk, eggs, chiles, and oil in a large bowl, just until moistened.

Pour the batter into the prepared baking dish. Let sit for 5 minutes.

Bake for 20 to 25 minutes or until a toothpick inserted in the center comes out clean.

Let cool slightly, then cut into squares. Serve warm.

 Letting the batter sit for five minutes before putting the cornbread in the oven will create a nice top crust with a bit of a crunch.

Cheddar Corn Bread

Cheddar cheese is a perfect match with corn bread.

Butter, for the baking dish
1 cup yellow cornmeal
1 cup all-purpose flour
1/4 cup granulated sugar
2 tsp. baking powder
1 tsp. baking soda
1 tsp. salt
1 cup shredded Cheddar cheese
1 cup buttermilk
2 large eggs
1/4 cup butter, melted and cooled
3 Hatch green chiles, roasted, peeled,
    stemmed, seeded, and chopped

Preheat the oven to 400 degrees. Lightly butter a 9-inch loaf pan. Set aside.

Combine the cornmeal, flour, sugar, baking powder, baking soda, and salt in a medium-size bowl. Stir in the cheese.

Whisk the buttermilk, eggs, and butter together in a separate medium-size bowl. Add this mixture to the dry ingredients. Stir just until blended. Mix in the chiles and transfer the batter to the prepared baking pan. Let sit for 5 minutes. Bake for 45 minutes or until it is a deep golden brown on top and a toothpick inserted in the center comes out clean.

Chile Corn Bread

This is not-your-average corn bread.

Butter, for the baking dish
1 cup yellow cornmeal
1 tsp. salt
1/2 tsp. baking soda
3/4 cup milk
1/2 cup Hatch green chiles, roasted, peeled,
    stemmed, seeded, and chopped
1/3 cup vegetable oil
2 medium eggs, beaten
1 (8.25 oz.) can cream style corn, drained
1-1/2 cups shredded Monterey Jack cheese

Preheat the oven to 350 degrees. Lightly butter a 9-inch square baking dish. Set aside.

Combine the cornmeal, salt, and baking soda in a medium-size bowl.

Put the milk and chiles in a blender. Blend until smooth. Pour this mixture into the dry ingredients. Add the oil and mix together.

Stir in the eggs, corn, and cheese. Mix well. Pour the batter into the prepared baking pan. Let sit for 5 minutes. Bake for 45 minutes or until a toothpick inserted in the center comes out clean.

Cheesy Chiles Cornbread

This cornbread is cheesy and a bit spicy due to the addition of Hatch chiles.

Butter and flour, for the baking dish
1 cup yellow cornmeal
3 tsp. baking powder
1 cup shredded Cheddar cheese
2 medium eggs
1/2 cup vegetable oil
1/2 cup sour cream
1 T. diced pimiento
2 Hatch green chiles, roasted, peeled,
    stemmed, seeded, and chopped
1 (8.25 oz.) can cream style corn, drained

Preheat the oven to 400 degrees. Lightly butter and flour a 9-inch square baking dish. Set aside.

Mix the cornmeal, baking powder, and cheese together in a large bowl, just until combined.

Whisk the eggs, oil, sour cream, pimiento, chiles, and corn together in a separate medium-size bowl until well combined.

Add this to the cornmeal mixture. Stir just until moistened.

Pour the batter into the prepared baking dish. Let sit for five minutes. Bake for 50 to 60 minutes or until a toothpick inserted in the center comes out clean.

Let cool on a wire rack for 10 minutes before removing from the pan.

This is sooo good warm out of the oven and slathered with butter.

Bacon Cornbread

Bacon adds a wonderful flavor, baked into the cornbread.

Butter and flour, for the baking dish
1 cup all-purpose flour
1 cup yellow cornmeal
1/4 cup granulated sugar
4 tsp. baking powder
2 medium eggs
4 T. milk
1 cup sour cream
1/4 cup butter, melted
1 (8.25 oz.) can cream style corn, drained
2 Hatch green chiles, roasted, peeled,
    stemmed, seeded, and chopped
4 slices bacon, crisp-cooked and crumbled

Preheat the oven to 350 degrees. Lightly butter and flour a 9-inch square baking dish. Set aside.

Combine the flour, cornmeal, sugar, and baking powder in a large bowl.

Whisk the eggs with the milk in a separate, medium-size bowl. Stir in the sour cream, melted butter, corn, and chiles.

Add the egg-sour cream mixture to the flour mixture. Blend thoroughly. Pour the batter into the prepared baking dish. Sprinkle the bacon over the batter. Let sit for five minutes. Bake for 45 minutes or until a toothpick inserted in the center comes out clean.

Let cool on a wire rack for 10 minutes before removing from the pan.

Cheesy Corn Muffins

These moist corn muffins are made with buttermilk, fresh corn, and two cheeses which are cubed, giving you a delicious cheesiness in every bite.

Butter, for the baking dish
1/2 cup granulated sugar
1/2 cup butter
5 medium eggs
1 cup buttermilk
2 Hatch green chiles, roasted, peeled,
    stemmed, seeded, and chopped
1-1/4 cups yellow cornmeal
1 cup all-purpose flour
2 tsp. baking powder
1/2 tsp. salt
1 cup fresh corn
1 cup cubed Monterey Jack cheese
1 cup cubed Cheddar cheese

Preheat the oven to 375 degrees. Lightly butter the bottoms and insides of a muffin pan or use paper cups. Set aside.

Cream the sugar and butter together in a large bowl.

Add the eggs, one at a time, beating after each addition.

Beat in the buttermilk and chiles.

Combine the cornmeal, flour, baking powder, and salt in a medium-size bowl.

Gradually add the cornmeal mixture to the sugar-buttermilk mixture and blend well. Fold in the corn and the Monterey Jack and Cheddar cheeses.

Fill the muffin cups 3/4 full. Let sit for 5 minutes. Bake for 20 to 25 minutes or until golden brown.

Corn Tortillas

Masa is a flour made from corn that has been dried and then ground into a powder. You can find it in the baking section of the grocery store.

>2 cups corn masa mix
>1-1/2 cups warm water
>2 Hatch green chiles, roasted, peeled,
>   stemmed, seeded, and finely chopped
>Flour, as needed

Combine the corn masa mix, water, and chiles in a medium-size bowl. Mix with your hands into a soft dough.

Turn the dough out on to a floured surface and knead it until smooth.

Using 3 T. as a measure, form the dough into balls. Keep them covered with a damp cloth.

Cut a large Zip-lock plastic bag open down both of the sides.

Place the balls, one at a time, on one side of the plastic, cover with the other side, and use a rolling pin to press out the tortilla.

Cook the tortillas, one at a time, on a hot comal or in a skillet until they are lightly browned on each side.

 A comal is a round, low-sided skillet—similar to a griddle—which is used to cook tortillas.

Flour Tortillas

Fresh, homemade flour tortillas are so much better than store-bought packaged tortillas, plus the Hatch chiles make them ever so much better.

> 3 cups all-purpose flour
> 3 tsp. baking powder
> 1 tsp. salt
> 4 T. vegetable oil
> 1 cup warm water
> 2 Hatch green chiles, roasted, peeled,
>   stemmed, seeded, and finely chopped
> Flour, as needed

Sift the flour, baking powder, and salt into a large bowl.

Add the oil, water, and chiles. Mix with your fingers until well blended.

Turn the dough out on to a floured surface and knead for 3 to 5 minutes or until it is soft and no longer sticky. Cover with a damp cloth and set aside for 20 to 30 minutes.

Divide the dough into 18 balls that are about 1-1/2 inches in diameter. Keep them covered with a damp cloth. Roll out each ball on a floured surface with a rolling pin into a circle about 6 inches in diameter and 1/8-inch thick.

Cook the tortillas, one at a time, on a hot comal or in a skillet until they are lightly browned on each side.

Salsas, Sauces, and Seasonings

Black Bean Salsa

This fresh salsa can also be served as a vegetable side dish.

1 avocado, peeled, pitted, and diced
3 T. fresh lime juice
1 large tomato, chopped
1/2 red bell pepper, diced
2 Hatch green chiles, roasted, peeled,
   stemmed, seeded, and chopped
1/2 red onion, finely chopped
2 T. olive oil
1/2 tsp. ground cumin
1/4 cup chopped cilantro
1 (15 oz.) can black beans,
   drained and rinsed
1/2 cup corn, cooked tender-crisp
Salt and freshly ground black pepper
Tortilla chips

Toss the avocado with the lime juice in a medium-size bowl.
Add the tomato, bell pepper, chiles, onion, oil, cumin, cilantro,
beans, corn, and the salt and pepper to taste. Cover and chill at
least 2 hours. Serve with tortilla chips.

Chile Salsa

This tomato salsa is delicious on top of burgers, tacos, or fajitas, and served on the side with quesadillas.

3 cups chopped tomatoes
3/4 cup chopped cilantro
3 T. fresh lime juice
2 Hatch green chiles, roasted, peeled,
    stemmed, seeded, and chopped
1-1/2 tsp. ground cumin
Salt and freshly ground black pepper
Tortilla chips

Combine the tomatoes, cilantro, lime juice, chiles, cumin, and the salt and pepper to taste in a medium-size bowl. Serve at room temperature with tortilla chips.

Garlic Salsa

This chunky salsa is perfect at parties.

4 ripe tomatoes, coarsely chopped
1/2 red onion, coarsely chopped
1/4 cup chopped cilantro
Juice of one lime
2 Hatch green chiles, roasted, peeled,
    stemmed, seeded, and coarsely chopped
2 garlic cloves, minced
Salt and freshly ground black pepper
Tortilla chips

Combine the tomatoes, onion, cilantro, lime juice, chiles, garlic, and the salt and pepper to taste in a medium-size bowl. Serve at room temperature with tortilla chips.

Chile-Corn Salsa

A nice crunchy salsa featuring tomatoes, chiles, corn, and red onion, seasoned with cumin and lime juice. This is also a perfect topping for steak tacos.

> 1 (10 oz.) bag frozen corn, thawed
>   and cooked tender-crisp
> 2 Hatch green chiles, roasted, peeled,
>   stemmed, seeded, and chopped
> 1/2 cup diced red onion
> 1 small tomato, chopped
> Juice of 2 limes
> 2 T. chopped cilantro
> 1 tsp. ground cumin
> Salt and freshly ground black pepper
> Tortilla chips

Combine the corn, chiles, onion, tomato, lime juice, cilantro, cumin, and the salt and pepper to taste in a medium-size bowl. Serve with tortilla chips.

Chile Sauce

*There are so many ways to use this sauce. It's terrific on top
of chicken or beef. A spoonful or two stirred into a bowl of chili
adds heat and zip. This is also great on Huevos Rancheros.*

1 medium onion, coarsely chopped
4 Hatch green chiles, roasted, peeled,
    stemmed, seeded, and chopped
8 Roma tomatoes, cored and coarsely chopped
10 garlic cloves
3 cups water
2 tsp. salt
1/2 tsp. black pepper
1 tsp. granulated sugar

Combine all the ingredients in a medium saucepan. Bring to
a boil, then reduce the heat and simmer for 20 minutes, stirring
occasionally.

Let cool, then pour the mixture into a blender and purée until
smooth. Strain.

*Never blend hot liquids. The steam can cause them
to explode out of the top of the blender. Let the
mixture cool before blending.*

Huevos Ranchero Sauce

This is a great topping for Huevos Rancheros in the morning, but it's great with everything else, too. Serve it over sunny-side up or over-easy eggs placed on a warm corn tortilla, or use it as a topping for a scrambled egg burrito or omelet.

8 slices bacon, diced
1 large onion, chopped
1 garlic clove, minced
4 Hatch green chiles, roasted, peeled,
   stemmed, seeded, and chopped
2 cups chopped tomatoes
1/2 tsp. salt
1/4 tsp. black pepper

Cook the bacon in a 12-inch skillet over medium-high heat until crisp. Remove and drain on paper towels. Set aside. Drain most of the bacon fat.

Add the onion to the skillet and sauté until tender. Add the garlic and chiles. Sauté for one more minute.

Stir in the tomatoes and bacon. Season with salt and pepper. Bring to a boil, then reduce the heat, cover, and simmer for 20 minutes, stirring occasionally.

Ranchero Sauce

You may want to double or triple this recipe. Ranchero Sauce is delicious with so many dishes and can be used as the base for many recipes.

> 1 T. olive oil
> 1 cup finely chopped onion
> 1 tsp. finely chopped garlic
> 4 medium tomatoes, peeled and diced
> 3 Hatch green chiles, roasted, peeled,
>   stemmed, seeded, and chopped
> 1 tsp. chopped cilantro
> 1/4 tsp. chili powder
> 1/4 cup chicken broth

Heat the oil in a 12-inch skillet over medium heat. Add the onion. Sauté until tender. Add the garlic and sauté for one more minute.

Stir in the tomatoes, chiles, cilantro, and chili powder. Add the broth and stir to mix. Bring to a boil, then reduce the heat and simmer for 10 to 15 minutes, stirring occasionally.

Tomato Sauce

Instead of using canned tomato sauce, make your own to add zip to any recipe that calls for tomato sauce. It's great over Huevos Rancheros, meatloaf, and stuffed peppers.

4 large tomatoes
2 T. butter
2 T. olive oil
1 large onion, chopped
2 garlic cloves, chopped
4 Hatch green chiles, roasted, peeled,
    stemmed, seeded, and chopped
1/3 cup fresh lime juice
1/2 cup chicken broth
1/2 tsp. salt
1/4 tsp. black pepper
1/4 tsp. Tabasco sauce
1/4 tsp. ground cumin
1/4 tsp. chili powder
1 T. chopped cilantro

Preheat the broiler. Place the tomatoes in a shallow baking pan 5 inches from the heat. Broil for 5 minutes, then turn over and broil on the other side for 3 minutes. Remove and let cool. Core, peel, coarsely chop, and place in a food processor, along with the juices. Set aside.

Melt the butter with the oil in a 12-inch skillet over medium heat. Add the onion. Sauté until tender. Add the garlic and chiles. Sauté for one more minute. Place the mixture in a food processor. Purée with the tomato mixture.

Return the mixture to the skillet. Stir in the lime juice, broth, salt, pepper, Tabasco sauce, cumin, chili powder, and cilantro. Bring to a boil, then reduce the heat and simmer for 30 minutes, stirring occasionally.

Tomatillo Sauce

You can use this creamy sauce for chicken verde, add it to tacos, or serve it as a salsa with tortilla chips.

8 tomatillos, husked, rinsed,
   cored, and coarsely chopped
1/4 cup water
1/3 cup cilantro
2 garlic cloves, chopped
1/2 cup chopped green onion
3 Hatch green chiles, roasted, peeled,
   stemmed, seeded, and chopped
1 tsp. granulated sugar
1 (8 oz.) container sour cream

Place the tomatillos and water in a medium-size saucepan. Cook over medium heat for 15 minutes or until the tomatillos are soft, stirring occasionally. Let cool.

Place the tomatillo mixture in a food processor. Add the cilantro, garlic, green onion, chiles, sugar, and sour cream. Purée until smooth.

Green Chile Sauce

What Hatch chile cookbook would be complete without a recipe for Green Chile Sauce? This is the classic, all-purpose sauce; it goes well with everything.

  1 T. vegetable oil
  1/3 cup finely chopped onion
  1 garlic clove, minced
  1 T. all-purpose flour
  2 cups chicken broth
  1 cup Hatch green chiles, roasted, peeled,
    stemmed, seeded, and chopped
  1 small tomato, peeled and chopped
  1/4 tsp. ground cumin
  Salt and freshly ground black pepper

Heat the oil in a 12-inch skillet over medium heat. Add the onion and sauté until tender. Add the garlic and sauté for one minute.

Reduce the heat to low and stir in the flour, blending well. Slowly add the broth, stirring to incorporate into the flour.

Add the chiles, tomato, and cumin. Bring to a boil, then reduce the heat and simmer for 15 minutes or until the sauce has thickened, stirring occasionally. Season with salt and pepper to taste.

Sour Cream Sauce

Perfect on fajitas or as a dollop on a bowl of chili.

1 (8 oz.) container sour cream
1 cup Hatch green chiles, roasted, peeled,
   stemmed, seeded, and finely chopped
1/4 cup finely chopped red onion
Zest and juice of one lime
Salt and freshly ground black pepper

Put the sour cream, chiles, and onion in a medium-size bowl. Zest and juice the lime into the mixture. Stir to mix. Season with salt and pepper to taste. Pour the mixture into a food processor or a blender and pulse a few times. Chill until ready to serve.

Avocado Pesto

Great on just about everything, from tacos and burgers to chicken and fish.

1/2 cup extra virgin olive oil
1/4 cup fresh lime juice
2 garlic cloves, chopped
1 avocado, peeled, pitted, and chopped
2 Hatch green chiles, roasted, peeled,
   stemmed, seeded, and chopped
1/4 cup pine nuts
1 tsp. ground cumin
Salt and freshly ground black pepper

Place the oil, lime juice, garlic, and avocado into a blender or a food processor. Purée at low speed for 2 minutes.

Add the chiles, pine nuts, cumin, and the salt and pepper to taste. Purée for 3 more minutes at medium speed.

Drinks and Desserts

Chile Hot Chocolate

Top this off with some whipped cream and a dusting of cinnamon and you're in Hatch Chile Hot Chocolate Heaven.

1 Hatch green chile, roasted, peeled,
   stemmed, seeded, and chopped
1/3 cup unsweetened cocoa powder
1/2 cup granulated sugar
Pinch of salt
1/3 cup boiling water
3-1/2 cups milk
3/4 tsp. vanilla extract
1/2 cup half-and-half

Mash the chile into a purée on a small plate. Set aside.

Combine the cocoa, sugar, and salt in a medium-size saucepan. Pour in the boiling water and the puréed chile. Bring to a low boil, stirring. Simmer and stir for 2 minutes, making sure that it doesn't scorch.

Stir in the milk and heat until almost boiling.

Remove the pan from the heat and add the vanilla extract.

Pour into mugs. Add equal amounts of the half-and-half to each mug.

Top with whipped cream and a dusting of cinnamon.

Vanilla-Avocado Milkshake

Cool and refreshing.

1 Hatch green chile, roasted, peeled,
    stemmed, seeded, and chopped
1 avocado, peeled, pitted, and chopped
3 cups milk
1 cup crushed ice
3/4 cup vanilla ice cream
6 T. granulated sugar

Place all the ingredients in a blender. Blend on high for one minute or until smooth. If you prefer a frappuccino, blend for 30 seconds.

Use any flavor ice cream to vary the taste. Use other fruit, such as strawberries, mangos, or pineapple. If making a frappuccino, top with whipped cream and a light dusting of ground cinnamon.

Piña Colada

Now what could be better than sipping a piña colada on a hot day?

Crushed ice cubes
1 cup rum
1 cup coconut cream
1/2 cup coconut milk
2 Hatch green chiles, roasted, peeled,
    stemmed, seeded, and chopped
1/2 cup fresh pineapple chunks

Fill the blender halfway full with ice. Add the rum, coconut cream, coconut milk, chiles, and pineapple. Purée until smooth.

Strawberry Daiquiri

Fruity and delicious.

1 pound fresh strawberries, stemmed and halved
1/2 cup granulated sugar
1/3 cup unsweetened pineapple juice
1 T. fresh lime juice
3/4 cup spiced rum
2 Hatch green chiles, roasted, peeled,
    stemmed, seeded, and chopped
Crushed ice

Place the strawberries and sugar in a blender. Blend until smooth. Strain, if desired.

Add the pineapple juice, lime juice, rum, and chiles. Pulse until combined. Serve over ice.

Chile Ice

Mix in some vodka and you have a Bloody Mary.

3 cups tomato juice
2 T. finely minced onion
2 T. Hatch green chiles, roasted, peeled,
    stemmed, seeded, and chopped
1 T. fresh lemon juice
1/2 tsp. finely minced basil
1 celery stalk, finely chopped
2 drops Tabasco sauce
2 T. finely minced parsley
4 parsley sprigs

Combine all the ingredients except the parsley in a medium-size saucepan. Bring to a boil, then reduce the heat, cover, and simmer for 5 minutes, stirring occasionally.

Strain the mixture into an 8-inch square pan. Stir in the minced parsley. Cover and freeze until solid.

When ready to serve, let stand at room temperature for 20 minutes, occasionally breaking up the mixture with a spoon.

Place the mixture in a medium-size bowl and beat with an electric mixer on low to medium speed until it is mushy but not melted. Spoon into glasses and garnish with a sprig of parsley.

Chile Chocolate Chip Cookies

This cookie is similar to traditional chocolate chip cookies, except it has Hatch chiles and cinnamon.

1 cup butter, softened
1/2 cup confectioners' sugar
2 tsp. ground cinnamon
1 tsp. vanilla extract
2 cups all-purpose flour
1 (12 oz.) bag semisweet chocolate chips, divided
2 Hatch green chiles, roasted, peeled,
    stemmed, seeded, and chopped

Preheat the oven to 350 degrees.

Cream the butter and sugar together in a large bowl until creamy and fluffy. Stir in the cinnamon and vanilla.

Gradually add the flour, mixing well. Add 1-1/2 cups of the chocolate chips and the chiles. Mix well, then roll the dough into 1-inch balls and place on an ungreased baking sheet.

Bake for 12 minutes or until golden brown. Remove from the oven and let cool.

While the cookies are cooling, place the remaining chocolate chips in a small bowl and heat in the microwave for 30 seconds or until completely melted.

Using a spoon, drizzle the chocolate over each cookie. Chill until the chocolate is set.

 To make **Quick Chocolate Chip Cookies**, *combine one (18 oz.) package refrigerated Chocolate Chip Cookie Dough with 2 roasted Hatch chiles, peeled, stemmed, seeded, and chopped. Follow the package directions to bake the cookies.*

Peach Cobbler

I love peach cobbler. The addition of Hatch chiles makes it ever so much better.

2 cups all-purpose flour
3 tsp. baking powder
1/2 tsp. salt
1/2 cup shortening
1 cup milk
2 T. water
1/2 cup granulated sugar, plus more for dusting
Zest and juice of one lemon
3 pints fresh peaches, peeled, pitted, and chopped
4 Hatch green chiles, roasted, peeled,
    stemmed, seeded, and chopped
1 cup sweetened condensed milk
Cool Whip topping

Preheat the oven to 450 degrees.

Sift the flour, baking powder, and salt into a medium-size bowl. Cut in the shortening and mix until the dough forms crumbs. Add the milk and mix until the dough forms a ball.

Knead the dough on a floured board until it is no longer sticky. Roll out the dough about 1/2-inch thick. Cut into 2-inch rounds. Set aside.

Mix the water, sugar, lemon zest, and juice together in a small bowl to make a syrup. Place the peaches and chiles in a large bowl. Sprinkle them with the syrup and stir to coat. Place this mixture into a 13 x 9 glass baking dish. Top with the dough rounds. Brush the dough with the sweetened condensed milk and dust with sugar.

Bake for 30 to 40 minutes or until the biscuits are golden brown. Serve warm, topped with Cool Whip.

Spice Cake

Be sure to use mild chiles in this cake.

Butter, for the baking dish
1-1/2 cups Hatch green chiles, roasted,
    peeled, stemmed, seeded, and chopped
2/3 cup milk
2-1/2 cups all-purpose flour
2 cups granulated sugar
1-1/2 tsp. baking soda
1/4 tsp. baking powder
1-1/2 tsp. salt
1 tsp. ground cinnamon
1/2 tsp. ground cloves
1/2 tsp. allspice
1/2 cup vegetable oil
2 large eggs
Confectioners' sugar

Preheat the oven to 350 degrees. Lightly butter a 13 x 9 glass baking dish. Set aside.

Place the chiles and milk in a blender. Purée until smooth, then pour into a large bowl. Add all the remaining ingredients except the confectioners' sugar. Blend for one minute on low speed with an electric mixer, then for 3 minutes on high speed, scraping the bowl occasionally.

Pour the batter into the prepared baking dish. Bake for 55 to 65 minutes or until a wooden toothpick inserted in the center comes out clean. Let cool before serving. Dust with confectioners' sugar.

The cake is an awful color green (from the chiles), so just get past that and enjoy this delicious cake.

Brownies

O.M.G. These are sooo good!!

    2 sticks unsalted butter, at room temperature
    1 cup bittersweet chocolate, chopped
    4 large eggs
    1/2 tsp. salt
    1 cup granulated sugar
    1 cup firmly packed dark brown sugar
    2 tsp. vanilla extract
    1/2 cup Hatch green chiles, roasted, peeled,
        stemmed, seeded, and chopped
    1 cup chopped pecans or walnuts
    1 cup all-purpose flour

Preheat the oven to 350 degrees. Line a 13 x 9 glass baking dish with parchment paper. Set aside.

Combine the butter and chocolate in a double boiler over medium heat, stirring until melted. Set aside.

Whisk the eggs together in a large bowl, then whisk in the salt, both sugars, and the vanilla extract. Stir in the chocolate mixture, then stir in the chiles and pecans.

Fold in the flour. Pour the batter in the prepared baking dish and spread evenly. Bake for 45 minutes or until the top has a shiny crust and the batter is firm.

Cool in the pan on a rack. Let cool completely before cutting.

Berry Good Cake

Fresh berries and chiles are a good combination.

1 cup butter, melted
2 cups all-purpose flour
4 tsp. baking powder
1 tsp. salt
2 cups granulated sugar
1-1/2 cups milk
3-1/2 cups fresh berries
1/2 cup Hatch chiles, roasted, peeled,
    stemmed, seeded, and chopped
2 T. granulated sugar
1 tsp. ground cinnamon
1/2 tsp. ground nutmeg
1/4 tsp. ground cloves

Preheat the oven to 350 degrees. Pour the melted butter into a 13 x 9 glass baking dish. Set aside.

Sift the flour, baking powder, and salt in a large bowl.

Add the 2 cups sugar, then the milk. Mix thoroughly. Pour the mixture into the prepared baking dish.

Place the berries and chiles on top of the batter.

Combine the 2 T. sugar, cinnamon, nutmeg, and cloves in a small bowl. Sprinkle over the cake. Bake for 45 minutes.

 The berries and chiles will sink and the batter will rise during baking. If desired, top the cake with a dusting of confectioners' sugar or whipped cream. Sprinkle lightly with powdered cinnamon.

Cherry-Chocolate Cake

Flavored with cherries and chiles, this chocolate cake is flourless.

1 cup dried cherries
1/4 cup Muscat or Moscato wine
Butter, for the baking dish
1/2 cup unsalted butter
1 (12 oz.) bag semisweet chocolate chips
6 large eggs, separated
3/4 cup granulated sugar, divided
1/4 cup cocoa powder
Pinch of salt
1/3 cup Hatch green chiles, roasted, peeled,
    stemmed, seeded, and finely chopped
Confectioners' sugar

Combine the cherries and Muscat in a shallow bowl. Stir well and let sit for two hours.

Preheat the oven to 350 degrees. Butter the interior sides of a 9-inch round springform pan. Place parchment paper on the bottom of the pan. Butter the top of the parchment paper. Set aside.

Melt the butter and chocolate in a double boiler over low heat, stirring frequently. When fully combined, remove the pan from the heat and let cool.

Beat the egg yolks and 1/2 cup of the sugar on medium-high speed in a medium-size bowl, until pale yellow and smooth.

Add 3 T. of the chocolate mixture and mix well.

Gradually add the remaining chocolate mixture. Add the cocoa powder. Mix until incorporated.

Beat the egg whites with an electric mixer in a medium-size bowl until medium peaks have formed. Slowly add the remaining sugar and a pinch of salt. Continue beating until stiff peaks have formed.

Mix 1/3 of the egg white mixture into the chocolate mixture until they are no streaks. Fold the remaining egg white mixture into the chocolate mixture in two batches. Do not over-mix.

Fold the cherries and chiles into the batter. Pour the batter into the prepared baking pan. Bake for 40 minutes or until the center has set.

Cool in the pan on a rack for 30 minutes. Run a knife around the edge of the cake to loosen it. Remove the sides of the pan and allow the cake to fully cool.

Dust with confectioners' sugar.

 If you'd like, you can serve this cake with a dollop of whipped cream with a maraschino cherry in the center.

Kahlúa Chocolate Cake

Two of my favorite things—Kahlúa and chocolate.

Butter, for the baking dish
8 medium eggs
1 pound bittersweet or semisweet
    chocolate, coarsely chopped
16 T. (2 sticks) unsalted butter,
    cut into one-half inch chunks
1/2 cup coffee liqueur (Kahlúa)
1/4 cup Hatch green chiles, roasted, peeled,
    stemmed, seeded, and finely chopped
Confectioners' sugar
Raspberry Sauce (optional / recipe follows)

Position an oven rack in the lower third of the oven. Preheat the oven to 325 degrees. Line the bottom of a 9-inch springform pan with parchment paper and lightly butter the sides. Set the pan on a wide sheet of heavy-duty aluminum foil and wrap the foil up the sides. Set the pan in a larger baking pan. Bring a pan of water to a boil. (This is for the water bath as the cake cooks in the oven.)

Place the eggs in a large bowl. Using a hand-held mixer, beat the eggs for 5 minutes at high speed until the volume doubles.

Melt the chocolate and butter with the Kahlúa in a large heatproof bowl set in a pan of barely simmering water.

Gently fold one-third of the egg mixture into the chocolate mixture with a rubber spatula until a few streaks of egg are still visible. Fold in half the remaining egg mixture in the same way.

Fold in the chiles, then fold the remaining egg mixture into the batter until it is completely incorporated.

Pour the batter into the prepared baking pan and smooth the surface with a spatula. Put the baking pan in the larger pan and pour boiling water into the larger pan halfway up the side of the springform pan. Bake for 22 to 25 minutes or until the center has risen slightly, the edges are just beginning to set, and a thin glazed crust has formed on the surface.

Remove the springform pan from the water bath and set it on a wire rack. Cool to room temperature, then cover and refrigerate overnight.

About 30 minutes before serving, remove the springform pan sides, invert the cake onto a sheet of waxed paper and peel off the parchment liner. Turn the cake right side up onto a serving platter. Do this quickly. Dust the cake lightly with confectioners' sugar. If planning to use the raspberry sauce, make this at the same time.

Raspberry Sauce

This is an optional sauce with whipped cream topping for the Kahlúa Chocolate Cake.

1 (10 oz.) package frozen raspberries, thawed
Granulated sugar, to taste, divided
1 cup heavy cream
1 tsp. vanilla extract

Drain the raspberries and reserve the juice. Place them in a food processor. Pulse briefly, but not until smooth. Press the purée through a strainer to remove the seeds. Add some of the reserved juice, if desired. Sweeten it to taste with the sugar. Cover and refrigerate until ready to serve.

Whip the cream with the vanilla extract and 2 tsp. sugar, or more to taste, in a medium-size bowl until the whipped cream is nearly stiff. Spoon some of the sauce onto a serving plate. Place a slice of cake on top of the sauce and put a dollop of whipped cream on the top of the cake.

Strawberry Chile Cheesecake

Cheesecake flavored with chiles and served with a strawberry chutney on top.

>3 cups chocolate graham crackers
>4 oz. butter, melted
>24 oz. cream cheese, softened
>8 oz. mascarpone cheese, softened
>1 cup granulated sugar
>2 tsp. vanilla extract
>2 T. fresh lemon juice
>4 medium eggs
>2 Hatch green chiles, roasted, peeled,
>   stemmed, seeded, and puréed
>**Strawberry Chutney**
> 1 cup strawberries, sliced
> 1/2 cup Hatch green chiles, roasted, peeled,
>   stemmed, seeded, and sliced
> 1 cup granulated sugar
> 1/4 cup water

Preheat the oven to 350 degrees. Place the graham crackers in a food processor. Drizzle in the melted butter while blending until the crust is moist but not wet. Pack the mixture into a 9-inch springform pan on the bottom and up the sides. Bake for 10 minutes. Remove from the oven and let cool. Reduce the temperature to 325 degrees.

Put the cream cheese, mascarpone cheese, sugar, vanilla, and lemon juice in a medium-size bowl. Beat with an electric mixer, scraping down the sides to incorporate well.

Add the eggs, one at a time, beating after each addition.

Remove one-third of the batter to a small bowl. Stir in the puréed chiles.

Beginning with the cream cheese batter, marble the two batter mixtures over the crust in the springform pan.

Wrap the springform pan securely with heavy-duty aluminum foil. (This will prevent water from seeping into the mixture when the pan is put in the water bath.)

Place the springform pan in a larger baking pan and pour hot water halfway up the sides. Loosely cover the cake with aluminum foil. Bake for one hour to one hour, 20 minutes or until the cake is set and the center just jiggles. Remove from the oven and let cool, then refrigerate.

An hour prior to serving, make the Strawberry Chutney. Combine the strawberries, sliced chiles, sugar, and water in a medium saucepan. Simmer for 10 to 15 minutes. Remove from the heat and cool in the refrigerator.

When ready to serve, plate the cheesecake and serve the chutney over the cheesecake.

Apple Pie

The sweetness of the apples contrasts beautifully with the spiciness of the Hatch chiles.

1 (15 oz.) box refrigerated pie crusts,
 containing two 11-inch rounds
7 medium-size tart apples, peeled, quartered,
 cored, and cut in one-half inch slices
3/4 cup granulated sugar
2 T. all-purpose flour
1 tsp. grated lemon peel
1 tsp. nutmeg
1/2 tsp. cinnamon
6 Hatch green chiles, roasted, peeled,
 stemmed, seeded, and chopped
1-1/2 T. butter

Position an oven rack at the lowest position. Preheat the oven to 425 degrees. Place one of the crusts into the bottom of a 9-inch pie pan, leaving a one-inch overhang.

Toss the apples with the sugar, flour, lemon peel, nutmeg, cinnamon, and chiles in a medium-size bowl.

Spoon the filling into the pie crust. Dot with butter. Top with the remaining pie crust, trimming the edges and fluting to fit the pan.

Bake for 40 to 50 minutes or until the apples are tender and the crust is golden brown.

Serve warm or at room temperature.

If the edges of the crust begin to brown too soon, cover them loosely with aluminum foil.

Index

About the Author

Gloria Chadwick fell in love with Hatch chiles at first bite, putting them into practically everything she ate and creating new recipes to feature them.

She lives in San Antonio, Texas and is the author of numerous books ranging from New Age and self-help titles to cookbooks and guides for writers. Please visit her blog to have a look at her books... http://chadwickpages.blogspot.com.

Made in the USA
Columbia, SC
23 December 2017